Stripes by Example

Brent Watson

Apress®

Stripes by Example

ISBN-13 (pbk): 978-1-4842-0981-3

ISBN-13 (electronic): 978-1-4842-0980-6

Library of Congress Control Number: 2015936618

Managing Director: Welmoed Spahr
Lead Editor: Steve Anglin
Technical Reviewer: Justin Lee
Editorial Board: Steve Anglin, Louise Corrigan, Jonathan Gennick, Robert Hutchinson, Michelle Lowman, James Markham, Susan McDermott, Matthew Moodie, Jeff Olson, Jeffrey Pepper, Douglas Pundick, Ben Renow-Clarke, Gwenan Spearing, Steve Weiss
Coordinating Editor: Mark Powers
Copy Editor: Kimberly Burton-Weisman
Compositor: SPi Global
Indexer: SPi Global
Artist: SPi Global

Distributed to the book trade worldwide by Springer Science+Business Media New York, 233 Spring Street, 6th Floor, New York, NY 10013. Phone 1-800-SPRINGER, fax (201) 348-4505, e-mail orders-ny@springer-sbm.com, or visit www.springeronline.com. Apress Media, LLC is a California LLC and the sole member (owner) is Springer Science + Business Media Finance Inc (SSBM Finance Inc). SSBM Finance Inc is a **Delaware** corporation.

For information on translations, please e-mail rights@apress.com, or visit www.apress.com.

Apress and friends of ED books may be purchased in bulk for academic, corporate, or promotional use. eBook versions and licenses are also available for most titles. For more information, reference our Special Bulk Sales–eBook Licensing web page at www.apress.com/bulk-sales.

Any source code or other supplementary material referenced by the author in this text is available to readers at www.apress.com/9781484209813. For detailed information about how to locate your book's source code, go to www.apress.com/source-code/.

Thanks
Kendra, Zoe, Isaac, and Jesus
in no particular order

Contents at a Glance

Contents

About the Author

Brent Watson is a Canadian developer currently based in New York City. He has been in the IT industry for 13 years, working on everything from Enterprise Java software to mobile applications in languages ranging from Java to Python to Go. Community has always been an important part of Brent's life, be it hosting meetups, running events for new startups, speaking at conferences, or doing a TEDx talk on how his skills as a software developer have made him a healthier person. In his spare time, Brent likes to spend time with his children, learn new technologies, watch kung fu movies, and cobble shoes.

About the Technical Reviewer

Justin Lee has been a Java developer since 1996 (and can still remember being excited about the upcoming release of the new Swing UI toolkit). Not counting occasional forays in to desktop development, Justin has spent the better part of the last 19 years doing server-side development, including building quasi-Java EE application servers and ORMs, and helping shepherd WebSockets support into GlassFish/ Grizzly and then into Java EE itself. He is currently a member of the MMS team at MongoDB, where he has worked on the Java driver, Morphia, and mongo-hadoop. He speaks as often as he can at conferences and user groups around the world, and blogs less than he intends at `antwerkz.com`. Follow Justin `@evanchooly`.

Acknowledgments

As you will see throughout this book, I dislike "filler" text. I've always thought that technical books are needlessly bloated. Acknowledgments fit into this category, so I will keep them brief so we can get on with what everyone came for. My thanks goes out to the Stripes community as a whole, without whom a book on Stripes would make no sense; to my wife and children, who offer huge support and great encouragement; to Justin Lee for doing a great job reviewing the material you are about to read; and lastly, to Steve, Mark, and the entire Apress publishing team for being a pleasure to work with.

Preface

Too many words. That's what most technical books contain.

How do you usually read a book like this one? If you're anything like me, you skim the text, and look at the code examples and try to figure them out. After you have an idea of how things work, you go try it yourself. Sound familiar? I thought so.

This book is written with exactly that learning method in mind. No filler, no empty explanations—just code. You won't be driving solo, however. Each code example is heavily annotated with comments and tips, so that you not only understand each snippet, but can also dive deeper if you so choose.

I hope you enjoy learning from this book as much as I have enjoyed writing it. But that's enough talk—let's get at it.

CHAPTER 1

Introduction to Stripes

Stripes is a web framework for the Java programming language. It was initially released in 2005 by Tim Fennell. Despite its growth and maturity, Stripes has always focused on two key principles: simplicity and ease of development. Stripes has also remained a solution for a single application tier: the web layer. Its purpose is to handle the interaction between a web browser and server-side Java code. To tie these concepts together, Stripes makes heavy use of Java annotations, which you will see as you learn the various features of Stripes.

As you progress through this book, you will find that Stripes provides a very simple learning path, where you do not need to understand the entire framework in order to use it. The concept of this book is exactly that—to get you using the framework and writing code immediately. You will be off and running in no time, and adding to your skill set as we progress. We will start with the basics of the framework to get you familiar with Stripes.

Stripes Development

Before we start, let's take a high-level look at how a Stripes application is structured. It is important to note that, thanks to annotations, Stripes does not require XML configuration like other Java web frameworks you might be familiar with. Yes, you read that correctly—no XML. The two parts of the Stripes framework that you will need to understand before starting with Stripes are ActionBeans and the Stripes tag library.

ActionBeans

When using Stripes, your server-side code will be referred to as *ActionBeans*. This is because your code must implement a provided interface—`net.sourceforge.stripes.action.ActionBean`. ActionBeans is covered in detail in Chapter 3, but as a sneak peek, we'll take a look at one right now. Listing 1-1 is an example of what an ActionBean might look like in an application.

Brent Watson, *Stripes by Example*, DOI 10.1007/978-1-4842-0980-6_1

Listing 1-1. Example ActionBean

```
import net.sourceforge.stripes.action.ActionBean;
import net.sourceforge.stripes.action.ActionBeanContext;

public class BlogActionBean implements ActionBean {
      ActionBeanContext context;

      public ActionBeanContext getContext() {
            return context;
      }

      public void setContext(ActionBeanContext context) {
            this.context = context;
      }

      public Resolution index(){
            return new ForwardResolution("blog.jsp");
      }

}
```

All of your ActionBeans will implement this Interface.

We will see what this ActionBeanContext code is in Chapter 3 – ActionBeans.

The final step is usually to display a .jsp page, which produces our output.

You will learn the details for ActionBean classes in the next few chapters, but for now, remember that *ActionBean* simply means server-side code.

Stripes Tag Library

Stripes also provides a set of tags that you can use in JSP files to help generate HTML code that is displayed to the user via their web browser. The purpose of the tags in Stripes is to interact with your ActionBean. This can mean displaying values that you set in your ActionBean, or specifying a value that will be sent to your ActionBean—for example, a form field that will be submitted to the server. The tag library also provides tags to allow you to navigate between ActionBeans and output error messages, and to perform many other utility functions.

An example JSP page that outputs a form might looks something like Listing 1-2.

Listing 1-2. Example JSP

```
<%@ taglib prefix="stripes"
        uri="http://stripes.sourceforge.net/stripes.tld" %>

<stripes:form beanclass="${actionBean.class}">

      <stripes:text name="yourName" />

</stripes:form>


<stripes:link beanclass="org.stripesbook.CustomersActionBean">
      View Customers
</stripes:link>
```

Include the Stripes tag library

Open form tag

Output a form field

Link to another ActionBean

ActionBeans will use JSP pages to render output, and that output will likely include links or forms that submit to other ActionBeans. The cycle between ActionBeans and JSP (HTML) output will continue like this indefinitely, as you can see in Figure 1-1.

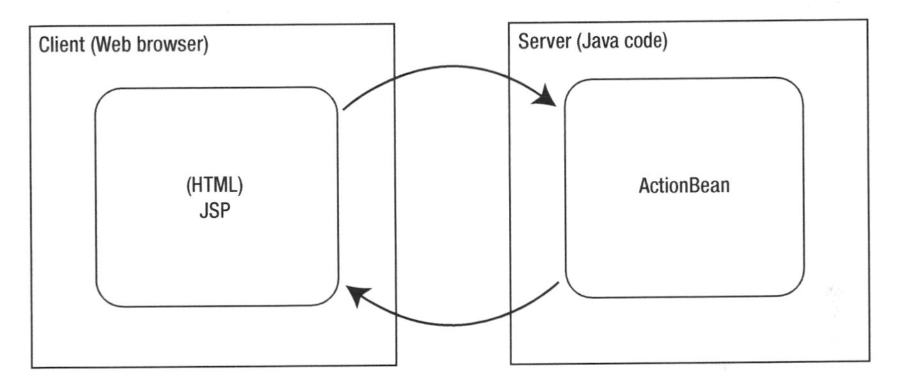

Figure 1-1. *ActionBean and JSP interaction*

Additional Features

In addition to ActionBean-to-JSP interaction, the Stripes framework contains many additional features. What makes Stripes a very easy framework to learn is that you don't have to know any of the details of the advanced features until you need them. You can be blissfully unaware about how Stripes validation works, or how interceptors are implemented, until you come to the point of wanting them in your application. Even when it's time to learn about these extra features, you will find that the principles of Stripes—easy to learn and fun to write—still apply.

Where to Go If You Need Help

As with any new topic that you learn, you will probably hit a snag or two on your journey to Stripes mastery. When this happens, your options are as follows: scream, cry, and pull out your hair (recommended); skim this book for additional references (also recommended); visit the Stripes framework web site (`www.stripesframework.org`); email the Stripes mailing list; or chat with an expert in the Stripes IRC channel (`irc.freenode.net#stripes`).

Review

We took a quick look at some Stripes basics: ActionBeans and JSPs. We will now explore these topics in detail. The latter half of this book will transition from the basic principles into building a number of Stripes applications, and thus interacting with other application layers and learning new features of the framework. We will conclude with the more advanced features of Stripes and I will suggest some best practices. Whether or not you have prior Java development experience, I promise that you will find Stripes development quick to learn and fun to do.

Before we start coding, we need to set up a new Stripes project. Let's do that now.

CHAPTER 2

Getting Started

If you have any background in Java development, the setup for Stripes should be simple and familiar. If, on the other hand, you are new to Java development, the instructions in this chapter are detailed enough to guide you through the process, step by step.

Download Java

If you are completely new to Java development, you will need to first install the Java Development Kit (JDK). This is the set of tools used to compile and run Java programs. Download and install this from the following web site: `www.oracle.com/technetwork/java/javase/downloads/index.html`.

Caution Be sure to install the JDK, not the JRE (Java Runtime Environment), which only allows you to run Java applications, not write and compile them.

Start a New Project

Figures 2-1 through 2-4 show how to set up a basic Stripes project using an IDE (Integrated Development Environment) called NetBeans. This book was written using NetBeans. NetBeans is free and can be downloaded from `www.netbeans.org`. Download either the Full version, or the Java EE version—either one will do.

1. Select New Project from the NetBeans File menu, as shown in Figure 2-1.

Brent Watson, *Stripes by Example*, DOI 10.1007/978-1-4842-0980-6_2

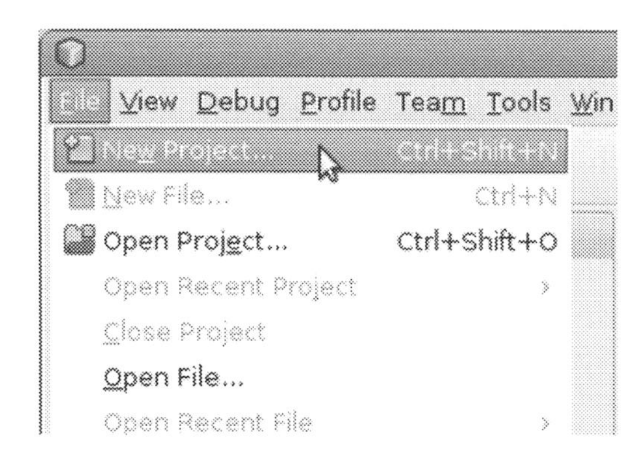

Figure 2-1. *New project setup*

2. Select Java Web ➤ Web Application, as shown in Figure 2-2.

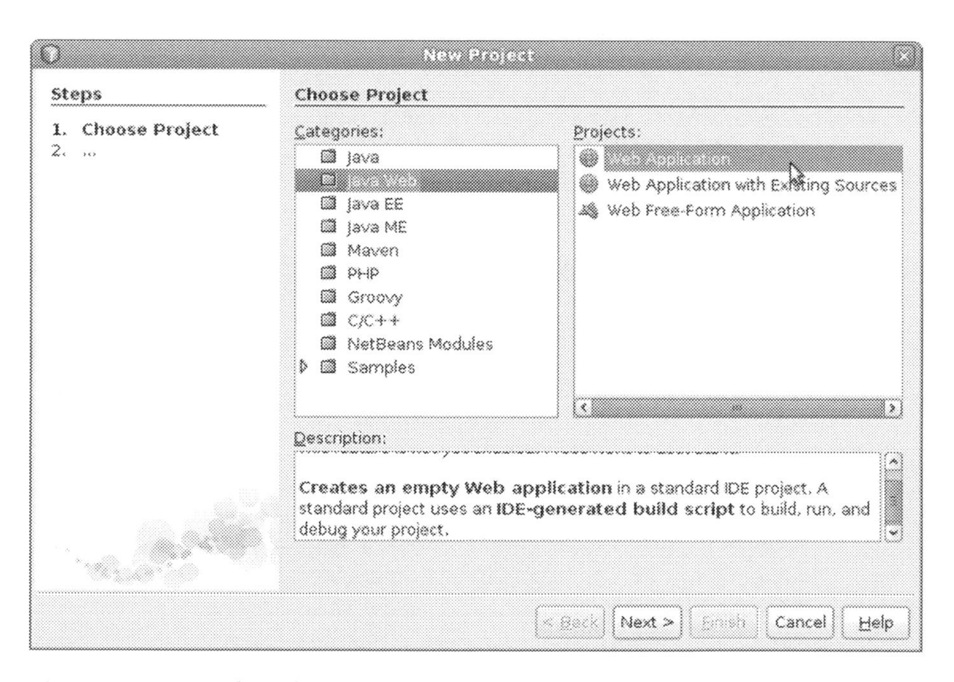

Figure 2-2. *New web application*

3. Give your project a name, such as StripesBook or StripesByExample, and set your project location. Here I use a Linux style path (see Figure 2-3). If you are on Windows, this would be a Windows path such as `c:\MyCode\StripesBook`.

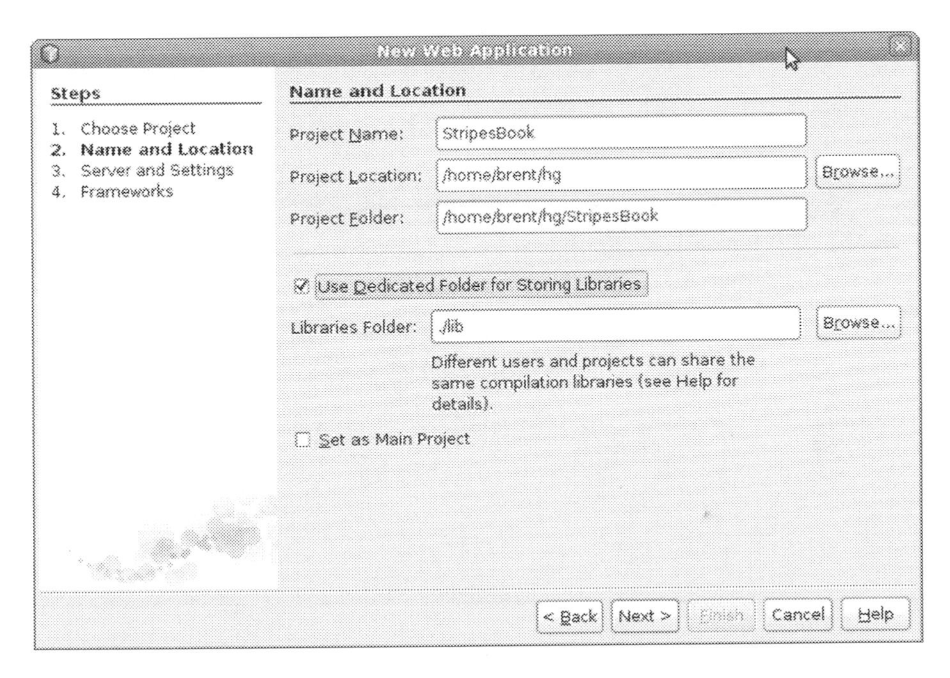

Figure 2-3. *Project properties*

4. Select an existing application server to run on. NetBeans ships with GlassFish; it is a very good, robust, free application server. So choose it, as shown in Figure 2-4.

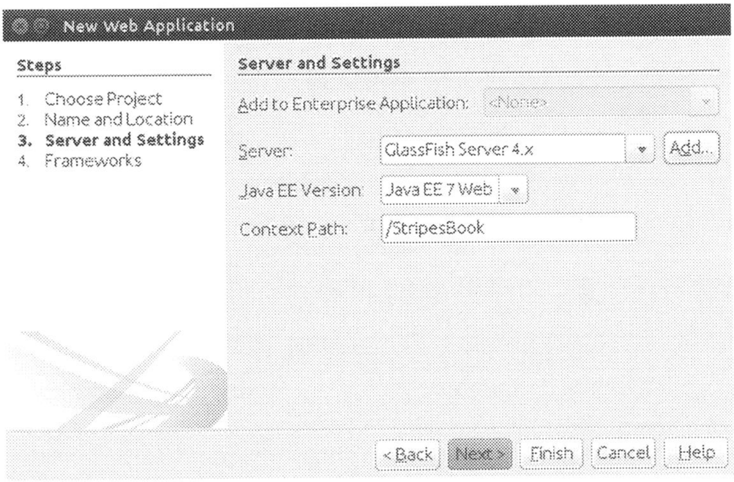

Figure 2-4. *Server settings*

▒ **Note** The Context Path (a.k.a. Context Root) will be part of the URL under which your application runs. For example, if your context path is `/stripesbook`, as in the preceding example, the path to your application will be `http://localhost:8080/`**`stripesbook`**.

---

5. You now have an empty Java web application. You can right-click the project name, and then click Run to launch your application. Once the project compiles and your application server starts, you should see a default Hello World web page.

The next step is to add the Stripes framework to the project. You have a few different options available to accomplish this.

Adding Stripes to Your Project

To add Stripes to an application, you can either manually download the files, or if you are familiar with a Java build framework called Maven2, you can optionally use it to download the files and their dependencies for you. If you have no experience with Maven2, I suggest downloading the files manually since this gives you a better understanding of what is going on.

Option 1: Manual File Downloads

You will now download Stripes.

1. Download the file `stripes-x.x.x.zip` from `https://github.com/StripesFramework/stripes/releases`.
2. This file contains the files that you need. Open the `stripes-x.x.x.zip` file with WinZip and extract `stripes.jar` and `commons-logging.jar` (located in the zip file's `/lib` directory).
3. Move or copy the extracted files (`stripes.jar` and `commons-logging.jar`) to your own project's `/lib` directory, as shown in Figure 2-5. (The `lib` directory is in the Project Folder that you defined when setting up the project in NetBeans).

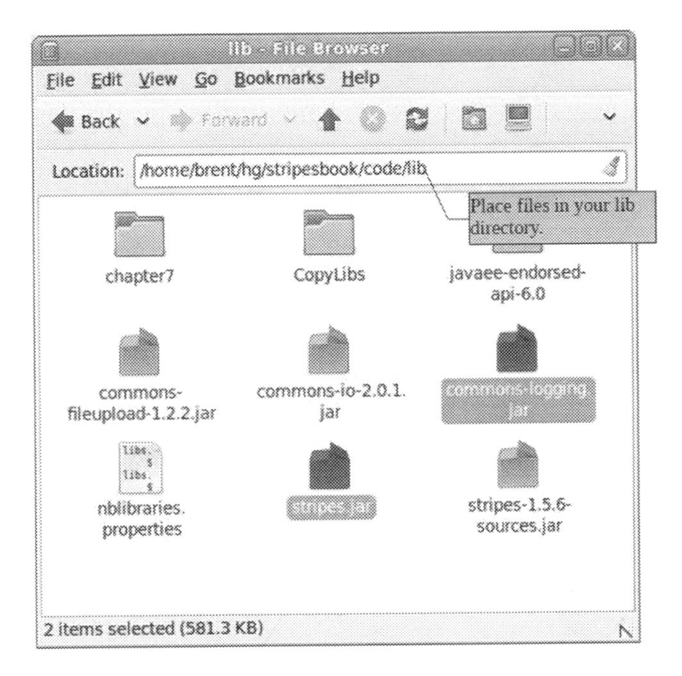

Figure 2-5. *Where to place your downloaded jar files*

■ **Note** While `stripes.jar` and `commons-logging.jar` are required, `stripes-x.x.x-sources.jar` is not. The latter is only used if you want to be able to browse Stripes source code from within NetBeans. `commons-fileupload-x.x.x.jar` *and* `commons-io-x.x.x.jar` will be used in Chapter 14. These additional jar files are not yet required.

---

4. You now need to add these jar files to your project in NetBeans. You do this by right-clicking the Libraries folder icon in NetBeans and selecting Add JAR/Folder. Select the jar files (`stripes.jar`, `commons-logging.jar`, etc., as shown in Figure 2-6) and then click Open.

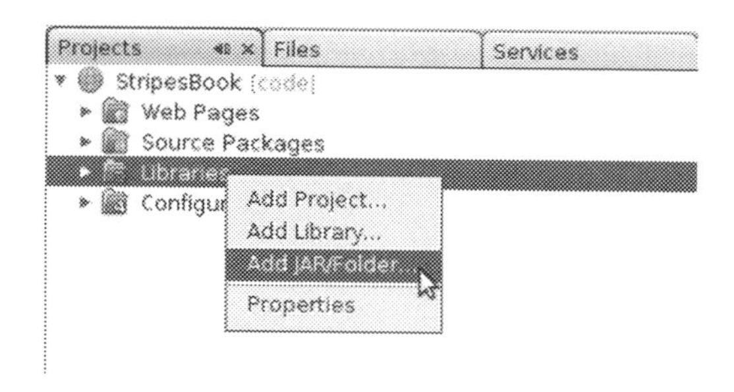

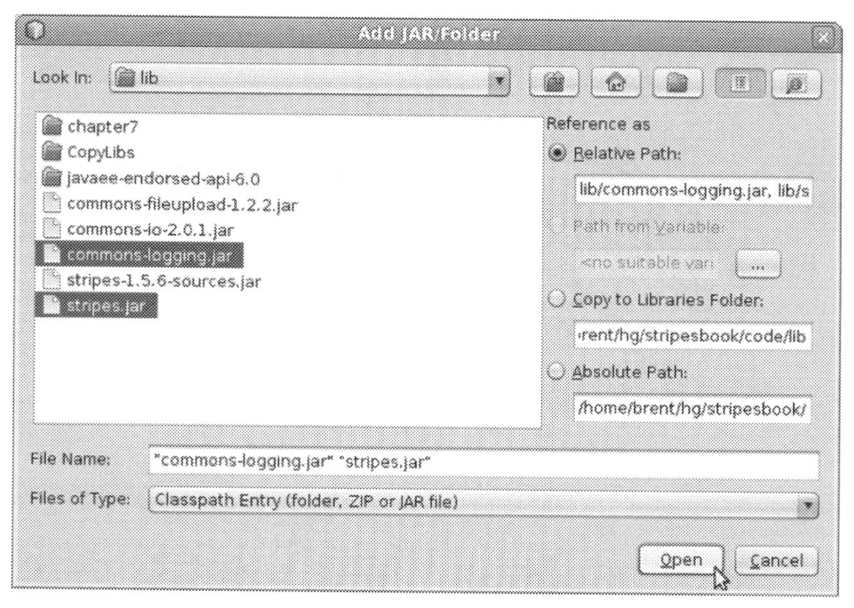

Figure 2-6. *Adding jar files to your project*

5. The last step is to copy the file `StripesResources.properties` from the zip file to your project's `/src/java` directory, as shown in Figure 2-7. This file contains Stripes settings for various output messages, such as errors and field labels.

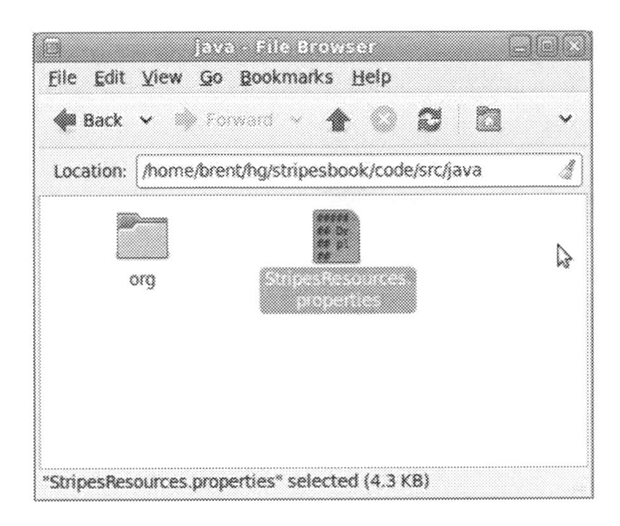

Figure 2-7. *Add StripesResources.properties to the project*

Option 2: Maven Setup

If you are a Maven user, you can add the dependency in Listing 2-1 to your `pom.xml` file for an existing web application to download the required Stripes jar files.

Listing 2-1. pom.xml dependencies

```
...

<dependency>
    <groupId>net.sourceforge.stripes</groupId>
    <artifactId>stripes</artifactId>
    <version>1.5.8</version>
</dependency>
```

This will cause Maven to download Stripes and its required dependencies for you when you build your application. If you are not a Maven user, don't worry—just follow Option 1 instead. Maven is outside of the scope of this book and it won't be referenced outside of this chapter.

Stripes web.xml Setup

Before you can write any code, you must set up Stripes. This chapter covers two methods available to set up a new Stripes project:

- The first option is for those new to Java development or those who do not use Maven. This first option requires you to configure your application manually by editing a file named `web.xml` (a file that holds server settings).
- Just as with the project setup in the last section, the second option requires a working knowledge of Maven2. The Maven option requires nearly no setup or configuration because it clones a template project with some specified settings.

However, as with the project setup, it can be advantageous to configure Stripes yourself because you will learn more about how it works.

Option 1: Manual web.xml Setup

When you created the Java web application, a `web.xml` file was created for you with a few default values (such as your default welcome page—usually `index.jsp`). Stripes is configured like most other Java web frameworks. It is set up to pass all URL requests of a specific pattern (e.g., `http://.../*.action`) through a *front controller*. In Stripes, the front controller is a class named `DispatcherServlet`.

1. Open your `web.xml` file. It can be found in the Configuration Files folder in NetBeans.
2. You can manually type Listing 2-2 into your `web.xml` file, or copy the text from either a digital copy of this book or from the Stripes web site at `www.stripesframework.org/display/stripes/Quick+Start+Guide`.

Listing 2-2. web.xml

```
<?xml version="1.0" encoding="UTF-8"?>

<web-app xmlns="http://java.sun.com/xml/ns/javaee"
         xmlns:xsi="http://www.w3.org/2001/XMLSchema-instance"
         xsi:schemaLocation="http://java.sun.com/xml/ns/javaee
         http://java.sun.com/xml/ns/javaee/web-app_3_0.xsd"
         version="3.0">

    <filter>
        <display-name>Stripes Filter</display-name>
        <filter-name>StripesFilter</filter-name>
        <filter-class>
                net.sourceforge.stripes.controller.StripesFilter
        </filter-class>
        <init-param>
            <param-name>ActionResolver.Packages</param-name>
            <param-value>
                org.stripesbook.chapter1,
                org.stripesbook.chapter2,
                org.stripesbook.chapterX...
                org.stripesbook.chapter15
            </param-value>
        </init-param>
    </filter>

    <filter-mapping>
        <filter-name>StripesFilter</filter-name>
        <url-pattern>*.jsp</url-pattern>
        <dispatcher>REQUEST</dispatcher>


    </filter-mapping>

    <filter-mapping>
        <filter-name>StripesFilter</filter-name>
        <servlet-name>StripesDispatcher</servlet-name>
        <dispatcher>REQUEST</dispatcher>
    </filter-mapping>

    <servlet>
        <servlet-name>StripesDispatcher</servlet-name>
        <servlet-class>
                net.sourceforge.stripes.controller.DispatcherServlet
        </servlet-class>
        <load-on-startup>1</load-on-startup>
    </servlet>

    <servlet-mapping>
        <servlet-name>StripesDispatcher</servlet-name>
        <url-pattern>*.action</url-pattern>
    </servlet-mapping>
    <servlet-mapping>
        <servlet-name>StripesDispatcher</servlet-name>
        <url-pattern>/action/*</url-pattern>
    </servlet-mapping>

</web-app>
```

These are the packages where our ActionBeans will be.

We can specify 1 or more packages here.

EXPERT TIP

Unlike most frameworks, Stripes not only uses a servlet as a front controller, but it also defines a filter class (`StripesFilter`) whose sole purpose is to ensure that all requests (even requests directly to JSP pages) go through the same `DispatcherServlet`. This is done so that all requests are able to take advantage of Stripes functionality, even if your server-side code is not being executed.

Option 2: Maven Setup

If you are a Maven user and have Maven2 installed (`http://maven.apache.org/`), follow these steps to create a new project. If you are not familiar with Maven, I suggest that you set up the project manually using Option 1 instead.

1. Download the Stripes QuickStart archetype jar file (`stripes-archetype-quickstart- X.X.jar`) from this URL: `http://sourceforge.net/projects/mvnstripes/`.

2. Run the command in Listing 2-3 to add the archetype to the list of available archetypes on your system.

Listing 2-3. Install the Stripes QuickStart Maven Archetype

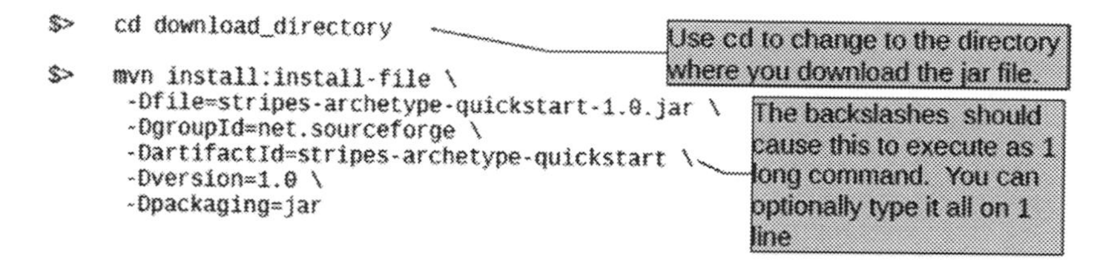

If successful, this should end with a "BUILD SUCCESSFUL" message.

Note that steps 1 and 2 only have to be performed once. Any new stripes project can now be created by following steps 3 and 4.

3. Use the new archetype to create a project (see Listing 2-4).

Listing 2-4. Use Maven archetype to Create a Stripes Project

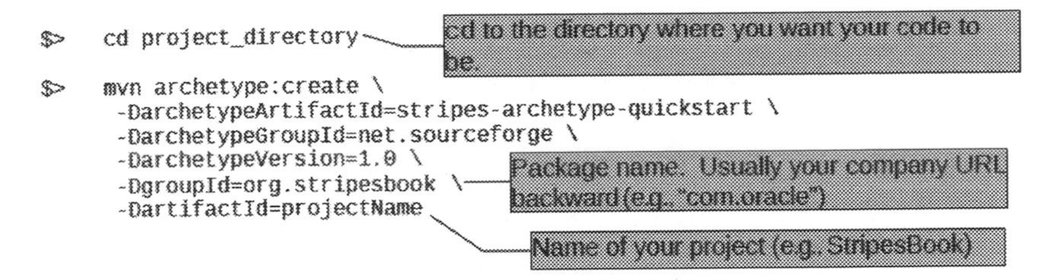

4. Open the project using your Java IDE (such as NetBeans by using the Open Project command), as shown in Figure 2-8.

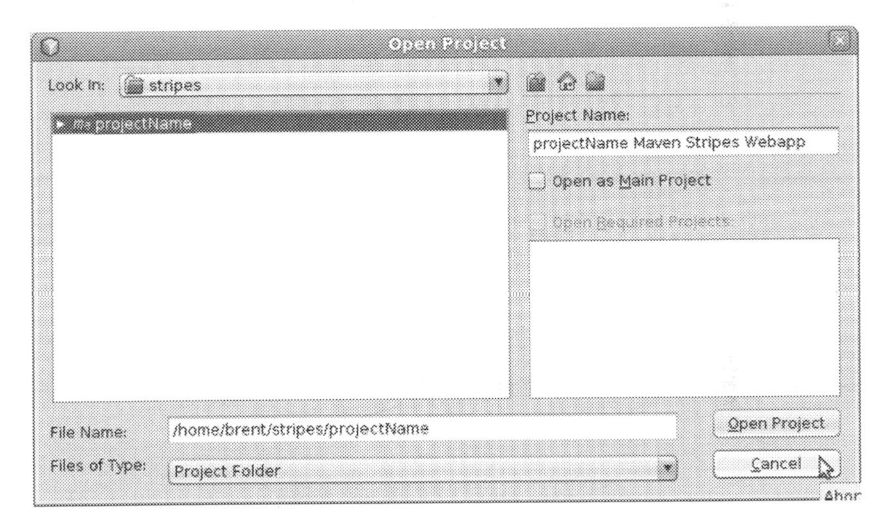

Figure 2-8. *Open the project*

If All Else Fails

Setting up any Java project takes a bit of effort. It becomes easier the more you do it, but can be a challenge the first time if the concepts are foreign. Understanding the project setup is important because it explains how Stripes works and how Stripes is configured. It also familiarizes you with where Stripes preferences are, which is good information to have because you will be modifying it in later chapters. Since the project setup only has to be done once, however, there is no reason for this to be something that stops you from progressing. If you have not been able to successfully set up a Stripes project, I provide a pre-setup project that you can download, unzip, and open (using File ➤ Open Project with the NetBeans IDE). This starter project can be downloaded from the following URL: `www.stripesbyexample.com/NewStripesApplication.zip` or from the Apress web site at `www.apress.com/9781484209813`.

Review

Your IDE is up and running. Your project is set up and ready. You have Stripes configured. You are now ready to start learning Stripes. We will start with ActionBeans—the cornerstone of building a Stripes application.

CHAPTER 3

ActionBeans

Now that your IDE is set up and you have all the files you need to build a Stripes application, you can build a fully working application. This chapter covers the main cornerstone of Stripes—the ActionBean. As you will see in this chapter, and throughout the rest of the book, you can't do much in Stripes without ActionBeans. This stuff is important and also relatively simple, so pay attention. You've already seen the ActionBean introduced earlier in this book. Here we will dive into all the available features and functions of ActionBean classes.

An Introduction to ActionBeans

In this example, you will see the basic setup for a Stripes ActionBean, and the basic annotations required to make it work. Think of ActionBeans as the code behind a web page. They do some processing magic and then display results to the user. They can also take input from the user (e.g., form submissions) and do processing based on that input. For those familiar with the MVC architecture pattern, ActionBeans are the "C" in MVC (i.e., the Controller).

Listing 3-1 shows the simplest ActionBean that you can create. It has no actual functionality.

Listing 3-1. DoesNothingActionBean.java

```
import net.sourceforge.stripes.action.ActionBean;
import net.sourceforge.stripes.action.ActionBeanContext;

public class DoesNothingActionBean implements ActionBean{
    private ActionBeanContext context;

    @Override
    public void setContext(ActionBeanContext context){
        this.context = context;
    }

    @Override
    public ActionBeanContext getContext() {
        return context;
    }

}
```

All ActionBeans must implement the ActionBean interface.

The ActionBean interface defines 2 methods: getContext() and setContext(), which get/set an instance of ActionBeanContext.

Brent Watson, *Stripes by Example*, DOI 10.1007/978-1-4842-0980-6_3

The purpose of showing this "Does Nothing" ActionBean is to note that the Stripes framework forces you to implement getter and setter methods for an `ActionBeanContext` local variable. The purpose of this setup is so that the Stripes framework can pass in the `ActionBeanContext` when your ActionBean is instantiated and executed.

`ActionBeanContext` provides access to all of the HTTP request/response objects. For example, the `HttpServletRequest`, `HttpServletReponse`, and also `ValidationError` and `Message` objects that are used to pass messages back to the user from the server. But that is too much information for Chapter 3. We will see these used more in Chapter 9.

Hiding the HTTP request/response-specific objects in an `ActionBeanContext` object gives you one gigantic benefit; you are now able to write methods in your ActionBeans like regular Java methods, and only worry about HTTP request cycle code if you need to.

Listing 3-2 shows a very simple "Hello World" ActionBean, cleverly named `HelloWorldActionBean.java`. Listing 3-3 will also highlight using JSP pages to output data from the ActionBean as HTML. JSP pages are covered in extensive detail in Chapter 5.

Listing 3-2. HelloWorldActionBean.java

```
import net.sourceforge.stripes.action.ActionBean;
import net.sourceforge.stripes.action.ActionBeanContext;
import net.sourceforge.stripes.action.DefaultHandler;
import net.sourceforge.stripes.action.ForwardResolution;
import net.sourceforge.stripes.action.Resolution;

public class HelloWorldActionBean implements ActionBean{

    private ActionBeanContext context;
    private String message;

    @Override
    public void setContext(ActionBeanContext context) {
        this.context = context;
    }

    @Override
    public ActionBeanContext getContext() {
        return context;
    }

    @DefaultHandler
    public Resolution sayHello(){
        message = "Hello World";
        return new ForwardResolution("/jsp/chapter3/helloworld.jsp");
    }

    public String getMessage() {
        return message;
    }

    public void setMessage(String message) {
        this.message = message;
    }
}
```

Again, all ActionBeans must implement this interface.

Class variables hold data that will be passed to a view (JSP) or passed into the ActionBean from a view (more in Chapter 3).

Here are the setContext() and getContext() methods again.

@DefaultHandler will make this the default method to be run when this ActionBean is invoked.

Here we set message to "Hello World" and return a ForwardResolution object containing the path to the JSP file that will display the message.

Variables used by the JSP pages must have a getter and setter methods or be marked public.

As you can see in Listing 3-2, we are returning a `ForwardResolution` class with a path to a file named `helloworld.jsp`. JSP files can be created anywhere within the `web` directory that was created by your IDE when you created your project. The format used throughout this book is to place this in a subfolder under `web` named `jsp`, followed by the chapter name. Now let's see how the JSP page has access to the fields defined in `HelloWorldActionBean.java` (see Listing 3-3).

Listing 3-3. helloworld.jsp

```
<html>
    <body>
        <p>Message: ${actionBean.message}</p>
    </body>
</html>
```

JSPs automatically have access to a variable named `actionBean`, which is a reference to the instance of your ActionBean.

`actionBean.message` will call `getMessage()` on your ActionBean, returning "Hello World".

Although this example seems simple, there is quite a bit going on here. Stripes is going to handle executing your `sayHello()` method at the appropriate time (you will soon see how this works), it will take care of directing output to a JSP page, and your variables will be available within the scope of that JSP page through a variable called `actionBean`.

Refactoring to Remove Duplication

The obvious next step is to move the `ActionBeanContext` code into a base class, which will then be used by all of our future ActionBeans that we write. This not only helps follow the DRY principle of software development (Don't Repeat Yourself), but also provides a central place to add additional common feature methods—for example, a `isUserLoggedIn()` method, a `getDatabaseFactory()` method, or even logging methods.

Performing this refactoring leaves you with two files: `BaseActionBean.java` and your new `ShorterHelloWorldActionBean.java` (see Listings 3-4 and 3-5, respectively).

Listing 3-4. BaseActionBean.java

```
package org.stripesbook.common;

import net.sourceforge.stripes.action.ActionBean;
import net.sourceforge.stripes.action.ActionBeanContext;

public abstract class BaseActionBean implements ActionBean {

    private ActionBeanContext context;

    @Override
    public void setContext(ActionBeanContext context) {
        this.context = context;
    }

    @Override
    public ActionBeanContext getContext() {
        return context;
    }
}
```

All of the ActionBeans that we write from this point forward will extend this class.

Listing 3-5. ShorterHelloWorldActionBean.java

```
public class ShorterHelloWorldActionBean extends BaseActionBean {
    private String message;

    @DefaultHandler
    public Resolution sayHello(){
        message = "Hello World";
        return new ForwardResolution("/jsp/chapter3/helloworld.jsp");
    }

    // Getters and Setters...

}
```

Ah, so much simpler.

Once executed, the output should appear as expected (see Figure 3-1).

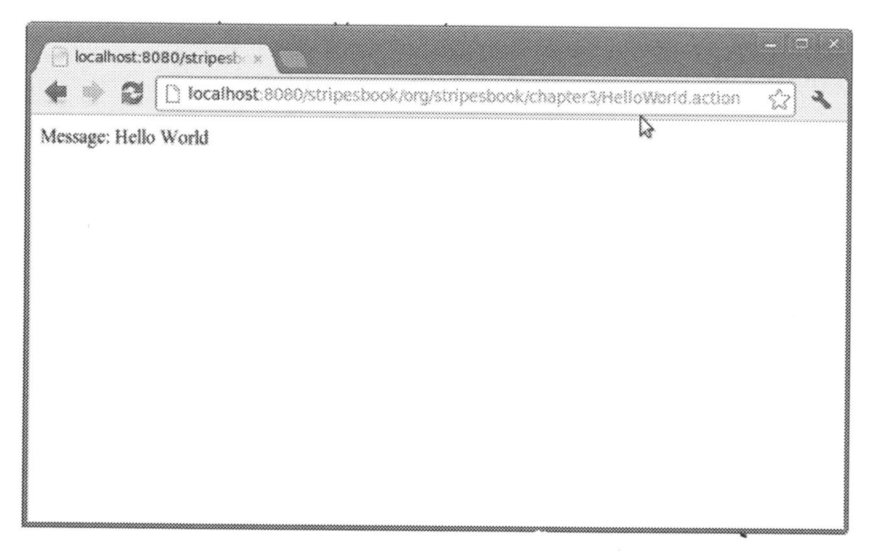

Figure 3-1. *The results of running the example*

Notice the URL in Figure 3-1. It shows the default URL format that Stripes will bind an ActionBean to. This takes the following format, assuming your package name has been defined in the ActionResolver.Packages setting in web.xml as described in Listing 2-4:

```
http://<server>:<port>/<context_root>/<actionbean_package>/<actionbean_
name(with "ActionBean" removed from the end)>.action
```

Allowing Stripes to produce default URLs such as these can actually be somewhat harmful for a number of reasons. First, this exposes too much internal information about your application, such as class names, package names, and the fact that you are using a specific framework. In addition, these URLs are not very user-friendly. Wouldn't something like `http://<server>:<port>/<context_root>/`**`customers`** be easier to remember, easier to communicate to others, and simply easier on the eyes? In the next chapter, you will see how to define your own URLs for an ActionBean.

Review

By this point, you should have a working Stripes project. You have seen what an ActionBean is—a Java class that implements the `net.sourceforge.stripes.action.ActionBean` interface along with the necessary `getContext()` and `setContext()` methods. And lastly, you have seen how to access ActionBean properties from a JSP page—by using `${actionBean.somePropertyName}`. We will continue by taking a look at the annotations used by Stripes to tie URLs to ActionBeans and methods.

CHAPTER 4

Mapping URLs to Methods

In this chapter, you will see how to use two of the most common annotations in the Stripes Framework: `@UrlBinding` and `@HandlesEvent`.

`@UrlBinding` is a *class*-level annotation that defines the base URL that is used to access an ActionBean. As we saw in Chapter 3, without an `@UrlBinding` annotation, the URL to access an ActionBean is the full package name and the ActionBean class with `ActionBean` trimmed from the end, and `.action` added (e.g., `http://localhost:8080/stripesbook/org/stripesbook/chapter3/HelloWorld.action`). However, by using `@UrlBinding`, we can change this to be a much nicer and more descriptive URL—any URL we choose, actually.

The `@HandlesEvent` annotation is a *method*-level annotation that is used to define the method to be executed, depending on the last part of the URL navigated to by the user. To sum it up, the combination of `@UrlBinding` and `@HandlesEvent` will define the URL-to-method mapping for an application. A method marked with `@DefaultHandler` will be executed if only the URL defined in `@UrlBinding` is browsed to by a user. This is sometimes referred to as an *index method*, and a common convention is to also name the `method index()`, though this is not required.

Using @HandlesEvent and @UrlBinding

Let's take a look at `@UrlBinding`, `@HandlesEvent`, and `@DefaultHandler` in action (see Listing 4-1).

Brent Watson, *Stripes by Example*, DOI 10.1007/978-1-4842-0980-6_4

Listing 4-1. UrlMappingActionBean.java

This will be the first part of the URL.

```
@UrlBinding("/action/UrlMapping")
public class UrlMappingActionBean extends BaseActionBean{

    @DefaultHandler
    public Resolution index(){
        return new ForwardResolution("/jsp/chapter4/index.jsp");
    }

    public Resolution eventOne(){
        return new ForwardResolution("/jsp/chapter4/another.jsp");
    }

    @HandlesEvent("eventtwo")
    public Resolution differentMethodName(){
        return new ForwardResolution("/jsp/chapter4/yetanother.jsp");
    }
}
```

We've seen this before. This is the default action (aka "Event") to perform. This will be run if the URL is http://../action/UrlMapping

This method will be executed, if the URL ends with "eventOne" (the method name). i.e., http://../action/UrlMapping/eventOne

This method will be executed if the URL is http://../action/UrlMapping/eventtwo

Let's go through the execution of this ActionBean and see how each of the three methods has been mapped to separate URLs.

Figure 4-1 shows how the `@DefaultHandler` annotation is used if you do not define a specific path in your URL. In the given example, our method name is `index()`, though it could be anything you wish as long as the `@DefaultHandler` annotation is applied to the method.

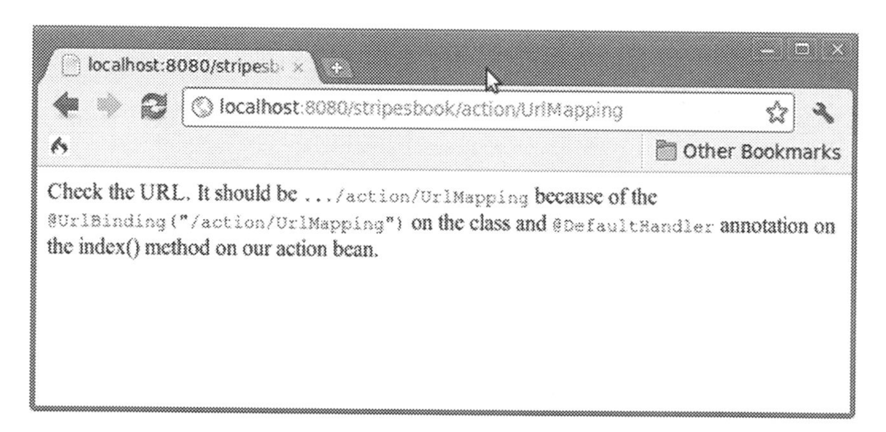

Figure 4-1. *URL mapped to the @DefaultHandler annotation*

Figure 4-2 shows the format of a URL to execute the second method in our code, `eventOne()`, which has no annotations applied to it. The URL, therefore, must match the method name exactly in order for that method to be called. And, yes, this is case sensitive.

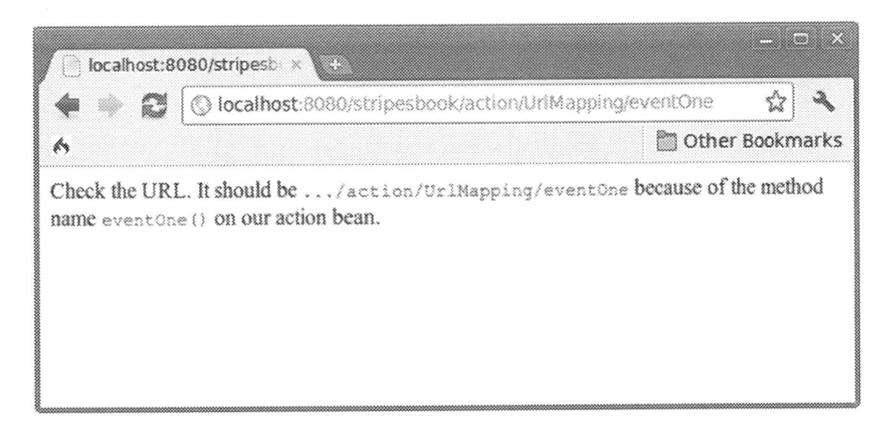

Figure 4-2. *A "raw" method name mapping, without any annotations applied*

A much better solution than exposing your internal method names is to use the `@HandlesEvent` annotation, as seen in Figure 4-3. Even though the method in Listing 4-1 was named `differentMethodName()`, here we see that the URL is mapped to `eventtwo`, which is the string provided in `@HandlesEvent`.

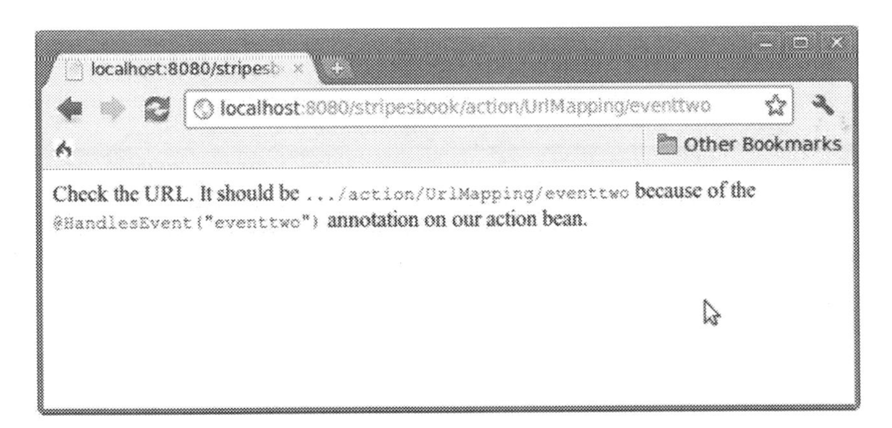

Figure 4-3. *A URL mapping using the @HandlesEvent annotation*

Linking to ActionBeans

Though we will look at JSP code more closely in subsequent chapters, Listing 4-2 shows how you create URLs to execute ActionBean methods, such as the preceding ones.

Listing 4-2. <a href> links

```
<%@ taglib prefix="stripes"
        uri="http://stripes.sourceforge.net/stripes.tld"%>

<h2>Chapter 4</h2>

<ul>
  <li>
   <stripes:link beanclass="org.stripesbook.chapter4.UrlMappingActionBean">
        UrlMappingActionBean#index
   </stripes:link>
  </li>
  <li>
    <stripes:link beanclass="org.stripesbook.chapter4.UrlMappingActionBean"
                  event="eventOne">
       UrlMappingActionBean#eventOne()
    </stripes:link>
  </li>
  <li>
    <stripes:link
        href="${pageContext.request.contextPath}/action/UrlMapping/eventtwo">
           UrlMappingActionBean#differentMethodName()
     </stripes:link>
  </li>
</ul>
```

Notice the <stripes:xxxx> tag being used. These stripes tags will be covered in more detail as we progress through the book – starting with Chapter 5

As an alternative to using beanclass, we can specify the actual URL using using this syntax.

EXPERT TIP

One of the strong points of Stripes is its very detailed error messages and stack traces. If you have been following along by coding your own examples, you might have seen some of these.

Here is one such example:

```
HTTP Status 500  - type Exception report

  description: The server encountered an internal error () that
prevented it from fulfilling this request.

  exception: net.sourceforge.stripes.exception.
ActionBeanNotFoundException: Could not locate an ActionBean that
is bound to the URL [/action/UrlMapping]. Common reasons for this
include mis-matched URLs and forgetting to implement ActionBean in
your class. Registered ActionBeans are:
{/org/stripesbook/chapter3/DoesNothing.action=class org.stripesbook.
chapter3.DoesNothingActionBean,
/org/stripesbook/chapter3/HelloWorld.action=class org.stripesbook.
chapter3.HelloWorldActionBean,
/controller/DefaultView.action=class net.sourceforge.stripes.
controller.DefaultViewActionBean,
```

```
/org/stripesbook/chapter3/ShorterHelloWorld.action/=class org.
stripesbook.chapter3.ShorterHelloWorldActionBean,
/org/stripesbook/chapter3/HelloWorld.action/=class org.stripesbook.
chapter3.HelloWorldActionBean,
/org/stripesbook/chapter3/DoesNothing.action/=class org.stripesbook.
chapter3.DoesNothingActionBean,
/org/stripesbook/chapter3/ShorterHelloWorld.action=class org.
stripesbook.chapter3.ShorterHelloWorldActionBean,
/controller/DefaultView.action/=class net.sourceforge.stripes.
controller.DefaultViewActionBean}
```

If you read such messages closely, you will notice that Stripes makes a few suggestions about where you may have gone astray. The preceding example gives the tip "`Common reasons for this include mis-matched URLs and forgetting to implement ActionBean in your class.`" It is clear that the framework contributors add messages such as these because the suggestions are common mistakes that developers will make when using the framework.

Review

We have now successfully mapped URLs to ActionBeans by using `@UrlBinding`. We have also seen both `@DefaultHandler` and `@HandlesEvent` used to link URLs to individual methods within our ActionBeans. The last thing we took a look at in this chapter was the `<stripes: link>` tag. The next chapter will continue on this topic by covering other available JSP tags.

CHAPTER 5

JSP Pages

This chapter is all about the "view" layer of an application. For Java web applications, that of course means `.jsp` files. The JavaServer Pages (JSPs) that we create will contain both HTML and a small amount of JSTL (tag library) code that outputs variables from our ActionBeans. We've already seen one example of this in Chapter 3's Listing 3-3.

We will also look at the Stripes *tag library*, which provides additional `<stripes:...>` tags, such as `<stripes:checkbox>` and `<stripes:link>`, on top of the `<c:...>` and `<fmt:...>` tags that you are used to using in JSP development.

Using JSP Pages with Stripes

Let's start with an example similar to what you've seen before, and then add more tags from there (see Listing 5-1).

Listing 5-1. JspExamplesActionBean — Version 1

```
@UrlBinding("/action/jsps")
public class JspExamplesActionBean extends BaseActionBean{
    private String bookTitle;

    @HandlesEvent("variables")
    public Resolution variables(){
        bookTitle = "Stripes by Example";
        return new ForwardResolution("/jsp/chapter5/variables.jsp");
    }

    //Getters and Setters...
    public String getBookTitle() {
        return bookTitle;
    }

    public void setBookTitle(String bookTitle) {
        this.bookTitle = bookTitle;
    }

}
```


Brent Watson, *Stripes by Example*, DOI 10.1007/978-1-4842-0980-6_5

▒ **Tip** `@HandlesEvent` is not actually required here, because if the annotation were missing, the method name would be used. However, it's a good convention to put `@HandlesEvent` annotations on any methods that will be accessed from a URL.

Here we see a simple ActionBean, not unlike what we have seen in previous chapters. The JSP to output the value of `bookTitle` should be familiar as well (see Listing 5-2).

Listing 5-2. variables.jsp

```
<html>
    <body>
        <p>Book Title: ${actionBean.bookTitle}</p>
    </body>
</html>
```

Now let's add something new to the ActionBean—a `List` of values (see Listing 5-3).

Listing 5-3. JspExamplesActionBean — Version 2

```
@UrlBinding("/action/jsps")
public class JspExamplesActionBean extends BaseActionBean{
    private String bookTitle;
    private List<String> bookTopics = new ArrayList<String>();

    @HandlesEvent("variables")
    public Resolution variables(){
        bookTitle = "Stripes by Example";
        return new ForwardResolution("/jsp/chapter5/variables.jsp");
    }

    @HandlesEvent("complex")
    public Resolution complexVariables(){
        bookTopics.add("Environment Setup");
        bookTopics.add("Getting Started with Stripes");
        bookTopics.add("Form data");
        bookTopics.add("...etc...");

        return new ForwardResolution("/jsp/chapter5/complexVariables.jsp");
    }

    //Getters and Setters...

}
```

Listing 5-4 shows how we loop through a list such as this.

Listing 5-4. complexVariables.jsp

```
<%@ taglib prefix="c" uri="http://java.sun.com/jsp/jstl/core" %>
<html>
    <body>
        <h2>Topics:</h2>
        <c:forEach items="${actionBean.bookTopics}" var="topic">
            <c:out value="${topic}" /><br />
        </c:forEach>
    </body>
</html>
```

EXPERT TIP

Using `${topic}` vs. `<c:out value="${topic}" />` would also work. I personally do not use `c:out`, but you may see it elsewhere.

Lists seem simple enough. How about `Maps` such as `HashMaps`? Let's add one to our ActionBean and JSP to see (Listings 5-5 and 5-6).

Listing 5-5. JspExamplesActionBean — Version 3

```
@UrlBinding("/action/jsps")
public class JspExamplesActionBean extends BaseActionBean{
    private String bookTitle;
    private List<String> bookTopics = new ArrayList<String>();
    private Map<String, String> chapters = new HashMap<String, String>();

    @HandlesEvent("variables")
    public Resolution variables(){
        bookTitle = "Stripes by Example";
        return new ForwardResolution("/jsp/chapter5/variables.jsp");
    }

    @HandlesEvent("complex")
    public Resolution complexVariables(){
        bookTopics.add("Environment Setup");
        bookTopics.add("Getting Started with Stripes");
        bookTopics.add("Form data");
        bookTopics.add("...etc...");

        chapters.put("Chapter1", "Introduction to Stripes");
        chapters.put("Chapter2", "Getting Started");
        chapters.put("Chapter3", "ActionBeans");
        chapters.put("Chapter4", "Mapping URLs");
        chapters.put("Chapter5", "JSPs");

        return new ForwardResolution("/jsp/chapter5/complexVariables.jsp");
    }

    //Getters and Setters...

}
```

Tip: Use a LinkedHashMap instead if you want to maintain the order you put them in.

Listing 5-6. complexVariables.jsp

```
<%@ taglib prefix="c" uri="http://java.sun.com/jsp/jstl/core" %>
<html>
    <body>
        <h2>Topics:</h2>
        <c:forEach items="${actionBean.bookTopics}" var="topic">
            <c:out value="${topic}" /><br />
        </c:forEach>
        <br  />

        <h2>All Chapters</h2>
        <table>
            <thead>
                <tr>
                    <th>Chapter #</th>
                    <th>Chapter Title</th>
                </tr>
            </thead>
            <tbody>
                <c:forEach items="${actionBean.chapters}" var="chapter">
                    <tr>
                        <td><c:out value="${chapter.key}" /></td>
                        <td><c:out value="${chapter.value}" /></td>
                    </tr>
                </c:forEach>
            </tbody>
        </table>

    </body>
</html>
```

This output would appear as expected—by displaying both the keys and values that we set in the HashMap, as shown in Figure 5-1.

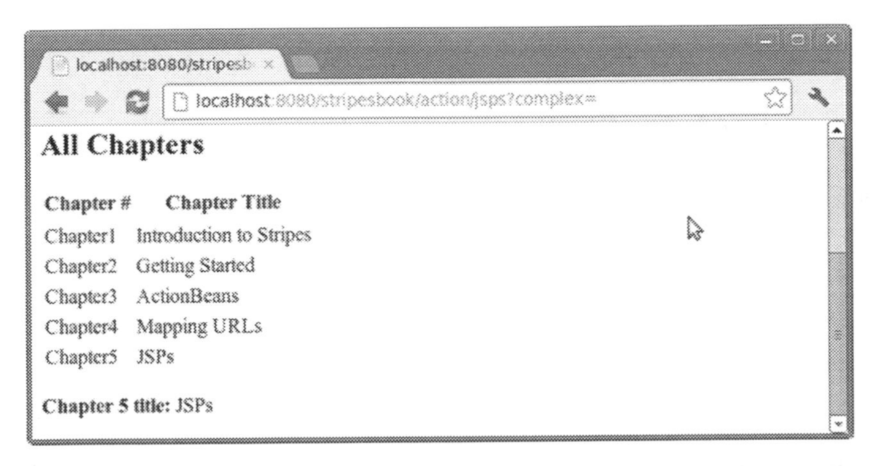

Figure 5-1. *complexVariables.jsp output showing data from JspExamplesActionBean.java*

The use of Maps also gives us the ability to reference a specific key in the Map (see Listing 5-7).

Listing 5-7. complexVariables.jsp

```
<%@ taglib prefix="c" uri="http://java.sun.com/jsp/jstl/core" %>

<html>
  ...
    <p><b>Chapter 5 title:</b> ${actionBean.chapters.Chapter5}</p>
  ...
</html>
```

The key in the HashMap

Ouputs "JSPs".

Now that we've seen how to work with ActionBean data using the standard core tag library (i.e., `<c:>` tags), let's take a look at the tag library that ships with Stripes (`<stripes:...>` tags). We will look at two types of tags that Stripes provides: tags that work with form data (input fields, check boxes, submit buttons, etc.) and tags that do not.

Stripes Tags

The ActionBean code required by the remaining JSPs in this chapter is very minimal. Let's make these changes first before seeing the rest of the JSP examples (see Listing 5-8).

Listing 5-8. JspExamplesActionBean — Final Version

```
@UrlBinding("/action/jsps")
public class JspExamplesActionBean extends BaseActionBean{
    private String bookTitle;
    private List<String> bookTopics = new ArrayList<String>();
    private Map<String, String> chapters = new HashMap<String, String>();
```

```
    @HandlesEvent("variables")
    public Resolution variables(){
        bookTitle = "Stripes by Example";
        return new ForwardResolution("/jsp/chapter5/variables.jsp");
    }

    @HandlesEvent("complex")
    public Resolution complexVariables(){
        bookTopics.add("Environment Setup");
        bookTopics.add("Getting Started with Stripes");
        bookTopics.add("Form data");
        bookTopics.add("...etc...");

        chapters.put("Chapter1", "Introduction to Stripes");
        chapters.put("Chapter2", "Getting Started");
        chapters.put("Chapter3", "ActionBeans");
        chapters.put("Chapter4", "Mapping URLs");
        return new ForwardResolution("/jsp/chapter5/complexVariables.jsp");
    }

    @HandlesEvent("tags")
    public Resolution stripesTagLib(){
        return new ForwardResolution("/jsp/chapter5/stripesTagLib.jsp");
    }

    @HandlesEvent("form")
    public Resolution stripesForm(){
        return new ForwardResolution("/jsp/chapter5/stripesForm.jsp");
    }

    // <editor-fold desc="Getters and Setters...">
```

The Stripes tag library contains primarily form fields. However, the `<stripes:link>` tag is not one of these, and is very useful, as shown in Listing 5-9.

Listing 5-9. stripesTagLib.jsp

```
<%@ taglib prefix="stripes"
           uri="http://stripes.sourceforge.net/stripes.tld"%>

<html>
 <body>

    <p>Create a link to go to the next example:</p>

    <stripes:link beanclass="org.stripesbook.chapter5.JspExamplesActionBean"
                  event="form">Next
```

```
    </stripes:link>

  </body>
</html>
```

Adding parameters to the generated URL can be done using `<stripes:param>` tags, embedded within `<stripes:link>`.

We can also take advantage of the `getClass()` method, which all Java objects have, and simplify the preceding code (see Listing 5-10).

Listing 5-10. stripesTagLib.jsp — Version 2

```
<%@ taglib prefix="stripes"
           uri="http://stripes.sourceforge.net/stripes.tld"%>

<html>
    <body>

      <p>Create a link to go to the next example:</p>

      <stripes:link beanclass="${actionBean.class}" event="form">
          Next
      </stripes:link>

    </body>
</html>
```

If it has not jumped out at you yet, the use of `${actionBean.something}` will call the getter method in the ActionBean.

Table 5-1 shows some examples.

Table 5-1. *Examples of Getter Method Calls on an ActionBean*

JSP Code	ActionBean Method Called
${actionBean.something}	getSomething()
${actionBean.myList}	getList()
${actionBean.class}	getClass()
${actionBean.context}	getContext()
${actionBean.loggedIn}	isLoggedIn()

This follows the JavaBean conventions laid out in the official Java specification (`http://www.oracle.com/technetwork/java/javase/tech/spec-136004.html`).

Stripes Form Tags

One important thing to remember about the Stripes *form* tags is that each tag must have a backing ActionBean property. For example, for a `<stripes:text name="bookTitle" />` tag in your ActionBean, you must have `private String bookTitle` in your Java code—along with getter and setter methods. Forgetting these will result in stack traces that reiterate this point.

Chapter 6 will focus on JSP-to-ActionBean interaction using `stripes:form` tags. Listing 5-11 is a taste of the available tags that Stripes provides for generating HTML form fields. The attributes are left blank in this example simply to ease readability.

Listing 5-11. stripesForm.jsp

```
<%@ taglib prefix="stripes"
        uri="http://stripes.sourceforge.net/stripes.tld"%>

<html>
    <body>

        <p>Form fields using stripes:form tags...</p>
        <stripes:form beanclass="${actionBean.class}">
            <stripes:text     name="" value="" />
            <stripes:checkbox name="" value="" />
            <stripes:radio    name="" value="" />
            <stripes:hidden   name="" value="" />
            <stripes:select   name="">
                <stripes:option value="1">Option 1</stripes:option>
                <stripes:option value="2">Option 2</stripes:option>
            </stripes:select>
            <stripes:button name="" value="Button" />
            <stripes:submit name="" value="Submit" />
        </stripes:form>

    </body>
</html>
```

Review

This chapter covered how to use the core JSTL tag library (namely, `<c:...>` tags), as well as some of the `<stripes:...>` tags that are available to us. As a repercussion of studying JSP tags, you were able to further your understanding of how ActionBean properties are accessed from JSP file—that is, via getter methods. In short, `${actionBean.someProperty}` must have a corresponding `getSomeProperty()` method in the ActionBean. The next chapter will pull together what you have learned thus far by building a small application. Also, watch for setter methods being used to accept form input!

CHAPTER 6

Forms

The purpose of most web applications is to take some form of user input, do processing around that input—such as saving, updating, or retrieving data—and then passing another view to the user. Wash, rinse, repeat.

The examples thus far have shown various features of the Stripes framework. The examples in this chapter will tie these concepts together.

An Example Application

We will create a small web application that stores data about DVDs (see Listing 6-1).

Listing 6-1. FormProcessingActionBean.java

```
@UrlBinding("/action/formprocessing")
public class FormProcessingActionBean extends BaseActionBean{

    private String dvdTitle;
    private double dvdCost;
    private String dvdGenre;
    private String message;

    @DefaultHandler
    public Resolution index(){
        return new ForwardResolution("/jsp/chapter6/form.jsp");
    }

    @HandlesEvent("save")
    public Resolution save(){
        message = "Submitted: " + dvdTitle +
                  " - a " + dvdGenre + " movie, " +
                  "which cost $" + dvdCost + ".";

        return new ForwardResolution("/jsp/chapter6/results.jsp");
    }

    //Getters and Setters...
```

Each of these will have a corresponding <stripes:...> input tag in the JSP.

The default action will be to display the form.

The form will submit to this method.

We will simply output a feedback message. More comon would be to save the data to a database.

Before seeing the JSP files that produce the input form and the results screen, let's look at the output from a user's perspective.

Figure 6-1 shows the input form that we will be creating as `form.jsp` in Listing 6-2. This is mapped to our `DefaultHandler` method.

Brent Watson, *Stripes by Example*, DOI 10.1007/978-1-4842-0980-6_6

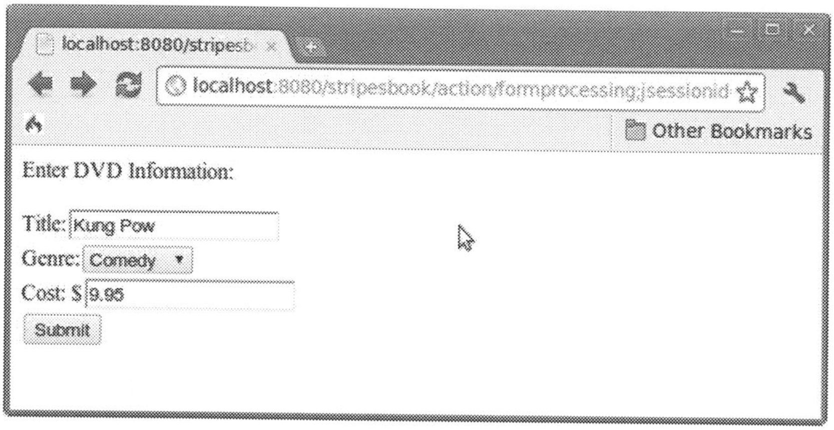

Figure 6-1. *Input form*

Figure 6-2 shows the results screen that we will be creating as `results.jsp` in Listing 6-3. The intent of this view is to show the data that is submitted from our form.

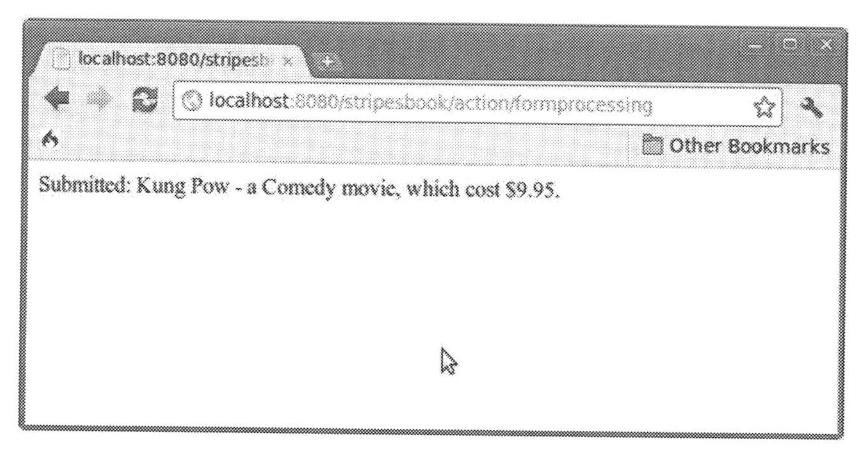

Figure 6-2. *Data passed from the input form, to the ActionBean, and then to results.jsp*

Now for the JSP files that create these screens (see Listings 6-2 and 6-3).

Listing 6-2. form.jsp

```
<%@ taglib prefix="stripes"
        uri="http://stripes.sourceforge.net/stripes.tld"%>

<html>
    <body>
        <p>Enter DVD Information:</p>
    <stripes:form beanclass="${actionBean.class}">
        Title:<stripes:text name="dvdTitle" /><br />

        Genre:<stripes:select name="dvdGenre">
            <stripes:option value="Comedy">Comedy</stripes:option>
            <stripes:option value="Romance">Romance</stripes:option>
            <stripes:option value="Action">Action</stripes:option>
            <stripes:option value="Horror">Horror</stripes:option>
            <stripes:option value="Other">Other</stripes:option>
        </stripes:select>
        <br />

        Cost: $<stripes:text name="dvdCost" /><br />

        <stripes:submit name="save" value="Submit" />
    </stripes:form>

    </body>

</html>
```

<stripes:option-collection> is also available; it outputs options from a backing List/Set in the ActionBean.

This will call the save event - @HandlesEvent("save") - on the ActionBean specified by the <stripes:form> tag. In this case, the same ActionBean that output this screen.

Listing 6-3. results.jsp

```
<html>
    <body>
        <p>${actionBean.message}</p>
    </body>
</html>
```

If you run the application at this point, you will see the screens shown earlier. Go ahead and try it out with a number of different values. Try adding another field yourself, such as `private int dvdRating;` to provide the ability to rate DVDs. Don't forget to add getter and setter methods for any new fields that you add.

Using Data Transfer Objects and Nested Properties

A more standard setup in a Java application is to use a Java object to wrap the input data, such as a `Dvd.java` class. This object could then be sent to a database layer to be inserted/updated, or it could be sent to a messaging queue to be processed, and so forth. This idea of using objects to store and transfer data between application tiers is a design pattern called a *data transfer object*, or a *transfer object*, or a *value object*—they all mean essentially the same thing. I will use *data transfer object*, or DTO, throughout the remainder of the examples in this book. When you see *DTO*, you know I am referring to a "container" object used simply for storing values.

Let's refactor the previous ActionBean to use a `Dvd.java` class to store the input data instead of having local fields. First, let's define what the DTO will look like (see Listing 6-4).

Listing 6-4. Dvd.java

```
public class Dvd {

    private String title;
    private double cost;
    private String genre;

    public Dvd() {
    }

    public double getCost() {
        return cost;
    }

    public void setCost(double cost) {
        this.cost = cost;
    }

    public String getGenre() {
        return genre;
    }

    public void setGenre(String genre) {
        this.genre = genre;
    }

    public String getTitle() {
        return title;
    }

    public void setTitle(String title) {
        this.title = title;
    }

}
```

Important: Stripes requires a no-arg constructor (inserted by the compiler by default if no other constructors are provided).

Now we can refactor our ActionBean to use the preceding `Dvd` DTO (see Listing 6-5).

Listing 6-5. FormProcessingDTOActionBean.java

```
@UrlBinding("/action/formprocessingdto")
public class FormProcessingDTOActionBean extends BaseActionBean{

    private Dvd dvd;
    private String message;

    @DefaultHandler
    public Resolution index(){
        return new ForwardResolution("/jsp/chapter6/dto/form.jsp");
    }
```

```
    public Resolution save(){
        message = "Submitted: " + dvd.getTitle() +
                  " - a " + dvd.getGenre() +
                  " movie, which cost $" + dvd.getCost() + ".";

        return new ForwardResolution("/jsp/chapter6/dto/results.jsp");
    }

    public Dvd getDvd() {
        return dvd;
    }

    public void setDvd(Dvd dvd) {
        this.dvd = dvd;
    }

    public String getMessage() {
        return message;
    }

    public void setMessage(String message) {
        this.message = message;
    }
```

In Listing 6-6 we will update our JSP form page to reference this new object.

Listing 6-6. dto/form.java

```
<%@ taglib prefix="stripes"
        uri="http://stripes.sourceforge.net/stripes.tld"%>

<html>
    <body>
        <p>Enter DVD Information:</p>
        <stripes:form beanclass="${actionBean.class}">
            Title:<stripes:text name="dvd.title" /><br />

            Genre:<stripes:select name="dvd.genre">
                <stripes:option value="Comedy">Comedy</stripes:option>
                <stripes:option value="Romance">Romance</stripes:option>
                <stripes:option value="Action">Action</stripes:option>
                <stripes:option value="Horror">Horror</stripes:option>
                <stripes:option value="Other">Other</stripes:option>
            </stripes:select>
            <br />

            Cost: $<stripes:text name="dvd.cost" /><br />
```

```
            <stripes:submit name="save" value="Submit" />
        </stripes:form>

    </body>
</html>
```

The JSP to output the message can remain the same, simply using `<p>$ {actionBean.message}</p>`. Though, we could refactor the JSP to reference the nested properties in the DVD DTO directly (see Listing 6-7).

Listing 6-7. dto/results2.java

```
<html>
    <body>
        <p>Submitted: ${actionBean.dvd.title} - a ${actionBean.dvd.genre}
            movie, which cost $${actionBean.dvd.cost}.</p>
    </body>
</html>
```

Complex Objects

In real-world applications, you will commonly see data stored in objects such as our `Dvd` class. Data transfer objects such as these can themselves contain other complex objects. Listings 6-8 and 6-9 are examples of this.

Listing 6-8. Customer.java

```
public class Customer {

    private String firstName;
    private String lastName;
    private Long customerId;
    private Address address;

    //Getters and Setters...
```

Listing 6-9. Address.java

```
public class Address {
    private String address1;
    private String address2;
    private String city;
    private String state;
    private String country;
    private String postalCode;

    // Getters and Setters...
```

JSP code to retrieve fields within a hierarchy of objects, such as a customer's postal code in our example, would be written like Listing 6-10.

Listing 6-10. customer.jsp

```
${actionBean.customer.address.postalCode}
```

This code would call the ActionBean's `getCustomer()` method (which returns a `Customer` object), and then that `Customer` object's `getAddress()` method (which returns the `Address` object), and then finally that `Address` object's `getPostalCode()` method.

You can nest objects as deeply as needed to represent what you are designing. The one thing to watch out for when doing this is a `null` reference. If any of the objects in the chain are `null`—meaning they have not yet been assigned to an actual instance of that object by using the `new` command—you will receive a `NullPointerException` when running your code.

Review

You have now seen the basics of how Stripes will be used in the wild—taking input data and providing output to a user. The interaction between multiple objects in this chapter is critical. Keeping Java classes and methods highly cohesive (that is, they should only be responsible for one thing) is very important when building an application, otherwise you will end up with a big mess of unmaintainable code (you have been warned!). Next, we continue our quest to build an end-to-end application by adding database capabilities.

CHAPTER 7

Working with Data

What good is data stored in DTOs and output as messages? Not much. This chapter will be an extension of the last chapter, but we will add a database backend to the application.

MySQL was used for the database in this chapter, though any database will work with Stripes. Stripes is a web framework only; it does not span into the database/ORM sector as some other frameworks do. As far as good design goes, it is recommended to have Controller and View code (ActionBeans and JSPs), and Model code that handles storing and retrieving data. As such, database code should be separated from code that uses the Stripes framework. Code components with the sole purpose of interacting with a database are called Data Access Objects (DAOs). DAOs can be referenced either directly from ActionBeans or from another layer of business logic, depending on the complexity of your application.

Note A JDBC jar file for your specific database vendor (MySQL, Oracle, PostgreSQL, etc.) is required for the examples in this chapter to actually function. The MySQL JDBC drivers are included with this book at `/lib/chapter7/mysql-connector-java-X.X.XX-bin.jar`.

Database Setup

Listing 7-1 is the SQL (DDL) used to create a database called `stripesbook`, containing one table—`dvds`—in a MySQL RDBMS. It can be pasted or typed into the `mysql.exe`/`mysql.sh` command line if you have MySQL installed and running on your system.

Listing 7-1. create_db.sql

```
create database stripesbook;

use `stripesbook`;
grant all privileges on stripesbook.* to 'stripesbook'@localhost identified
by 'password';
```


Brent Watson, *Stripes by Example*, DOI 10.1007/978-1-4842-0980-6_7

```
CREATE TABLE `dvds` (
  `id` INTEGER  NOT NULL AUTO_INCREMENT,
  `title` TEXT  NOT NULL,
  `genre` TEXT,
  `cost` FLOAT,
  PRIMARY KEY (`id`)
);

commit;
```

JDBC DAO

Next, let's create a DAO class with select and insert methods that interact with this database, as shown in Listing 7-2. I will repeat that this is pure Java code that has nothing to do with the Stripes framework.

This class will be *used* by our ActionBean. If you don't understand JDBC (Java Database Connectivity) code, don't worry too much about it because it is outside the scope of this book.

Listing 7-2. DvdDAO.java

```
package org.stripesbook.chapter7;

import java.sql.Connection;
import java.sql.DriverManager;
import java.sql.PreparedStatement;
import java.sql.ResultSet;
import java.sql.SQLException;
import java.sql.Statement;
import java.util.ArrayList;
import java.util.List;

public class DvdDAO {
    //DB Connection
    private Connection connection;

    //INSERT SQL
    private static final String insertSql =
        "INSERT INTO dvds (title, genre, cost) VALUES (?, ?, ?)";

    //SELECT SQL
    private static final String selectAllSql = "SELECT * FROM dvds";

    /**
     * Insert a DVD
     */
```

```
public void insert(Dvd dvd){
    Connection conn = null;
    PreparedStatement stmt = null;
    try {
        conn = getConnection();
        stmt = conn.prepareStatement(insertSql);
        stmt.setString(1, dvd.getTitle());
        stmt.setString(2, dvd.getGenre());
        stmt.setDouble(3, dvd.getCost());
        stmt.execute();
    } catch (SQLException ex) {
        ex.printStackTrace(System.err);
    } finally{
        closeAll(null, stmt, conn);
    }

}

/**
 * Select all DVD records
 */
public List<Dvd> selectAll(){
    List<Dvd> dvds = new ArrayList<Dvd>();

    Connection conn = null;
    Statement stmt = null;
    ResultSet resultSet;
    try {
        conn = getConnection();
        stmt = conn.createStatement();
        resultSet = stmt.executeQuery(selectAllSql);
        while(resultSet.next()){
            String title = resultSet.getString("title");
            String genre = resultSet.getString("genre");
            double cost = resultSet.getDouble("cost");
            Dvd dvd = new Dvd(title, cost, genre);
            dvds.add(dvd);
        }
    } catch (SQLException ex) {
        ex.printStackTrace(System.err);
    } finally{
        closeAll(null, stmt, conn);
    }
    return dvds;
}
```

```
    private Connection getConnection() {
        if(connection==null){
            String dbUrl = "jdbc:mysql://localhost/stripesbook";
            try{

                connection = DriverManager.getConnection(dbUrl, "stripesbook",
                             "password");

            } catch(Exception ex){
                ex.printStackTrace(System.err);
            }
        }
        return connection;
    }

    private void closeAll(ResultSet rs, Statement stmt, Connection conn) {
        try{
            if(rs!=null){
                rs.close();
            }
            if(stmt!=null){
                stmt.close();
            }
            if(conn!=null){
                conn.close();
            }
        } catch(SQLException ex){
            ex.printStackTrace(System.err);
        }
    }
}
```

That's a lot of code! In the "real world" of application development with Java, you would use a database framework such as Hibernate or Spring to ease this burden. For our purposes, writing the low-level JDBC saves us from explaining another framework.

ActionBean-DAO Interaction

Now let's refactor the ActionBean to store DVD data in our MySQL database by using the preceding DvdDAO class (see Listing 7-3).

Listing 7-3. SavingDataActionBean.java

```
@UrlBinding("/action/savingdata")
public class SavingDataActionBean extends BaseActionBean {
    private List<Dvd> dvds;  // Will contain existing DVDs.
    private Dvd newDvd;      // Will take data to be saved.

    @DefaultHandler
    public Resolution index(){
        DvdDAO dvdDAO = new DvdDAO();
        dvds = dvdDAO.selectAll();
        return new ForwardResolution("/jsp/chapter7/dvds.jsp");
    }

    @HandlesEvent("save")
    public Resolution save(){
        DvdDAO dvdDAO = new DvdDAO();
        dvdDAO.insert(newDvd);

        return new RedirectResolution(SavingDataActionBean.class);
    }

    // Getters and Setters...
```

Index method will get all existing DVDs from the database.

dvds.jsp will list the DVDs and display a form allowing the user to add new ones.

RedirectResolution redirects to another ActionBeans (HTTP 302 redirect).

this.getClass() would also work here. No event is specified, so the index() method will be executed.

This is our first look at `RedirectResolution`. It, along with `ForwardResolution`, implements the `Resolution` interface. Chapter 10 will cover resolutions in more detail. For now, it's enough to know that `ForwardResolution` specifies which JSP to "forward" the ActionBean data to for display, and that `RedirectResolution` is a way to perform an HTTP redirect to another page—useful when performing an event with no output or when errors occur.

The JSP code should be relatively familiar looking by now, so take a look at Listing 7-4.

Listing 7-4. dvds.jsp

```
<%@ taglib prefix="c" uri="http://java.sun.com/jsp/jstl/core" %>
<%@ taglib prefix="stripes"
        uri="http://stripes.sourceforge.net/stripes.tld"%>

<html>
    <body>
        <h1>DVD Collection:</h1>
        <c:if test="${actionBean.dvds!=null}">
            <table border="1">
                <thead>
                    <tr>
                        <th>Title</th>
                        <th>Genre</th>
                        <th>Cost</th>
                    </tr>
                </thead>
                <tbody>
                    <c:forEach items="${actionBean.dvds}" var="dvd">
```

```
                        <tr>
                            <td>${dvd.title}</td>
                            <td>${dvd.genre}</td>
                            <td>${dvd.cost}</td>
                        </tr>
                    </c:forEach>
                </tbody>
            </table>
        </c:if>
        <br />
        <fieldset>
            <legend>New DVD</legend>

            <stripes:form beanclass="${actionBean.class}">
                Title:<stripes:text name="newDvd.title" /><br />

                Genre:<stripes:select name="newDvd.genre">
                    <stripes:option value="Comedy">Comedy</stripes:option>
                    <stripes:option value="Romance">Romance</stripes:option>
                    <stripes:option value="Action">Action</stripes:option>
                    <stripes:option value="Horror">Horror</stripes:option>
                    <stripes:option value="Other">Other</stripes:option>
                </stripes:select><br />

                Cost: $<stripes:text name="newDvd.cost" /><br />

                <stripes:submit name="save" value="Submit" />
            </stripes:form>
        </fieldset>

    </body>

</html>
```

The resulting web site from the preceding code is now functional. Let's take a look. The first screen you will see is shown in Figure 7-1.

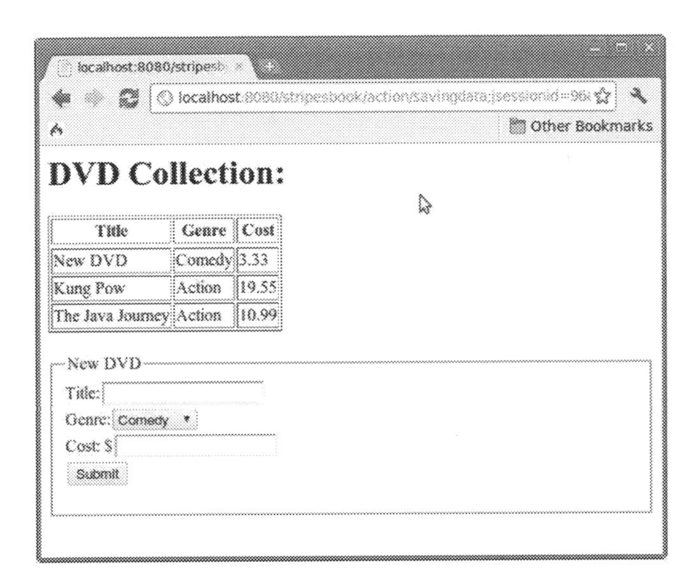

Figure 7-1. *Initial output of dvds.jsp when the page is first loaded*

You can then fill in the form and submit it, as shown in Figure 7-2.

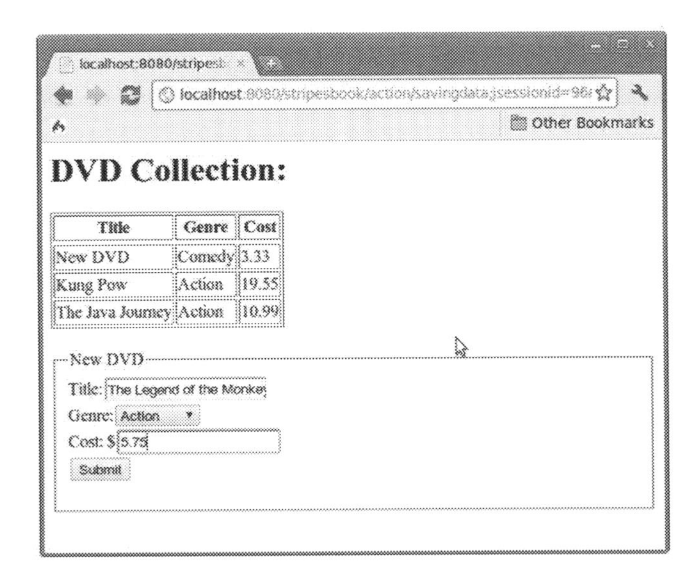

Figure 7-2. *Fill out the data and then hit Submit on the form*

Finally, the new data from the form is added to the database (see Figure 7-3).

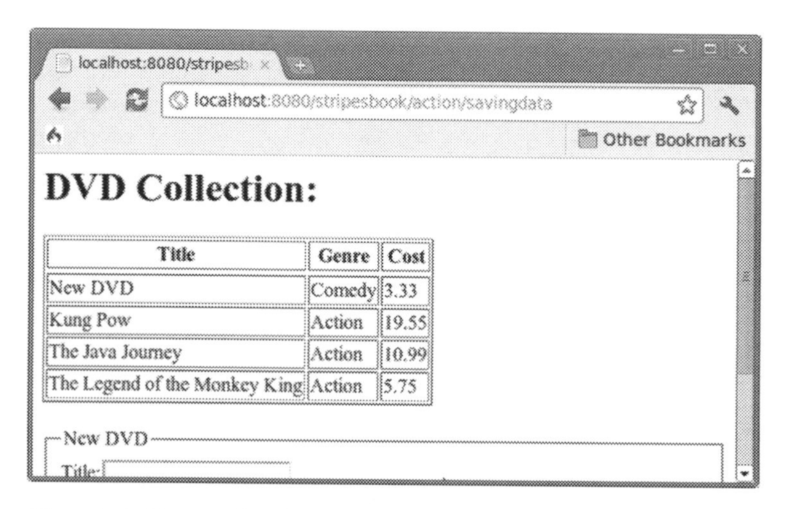

Figure 7-3. *The new data has been added to the database and is returned by our DVDs query*

And there you have it—a functional application. Though small, it does its job. In the next chapter, you will make a slightly larger application, with multiple ActionBeans and multiple JSP pages that must interact with each other.

Review

Although this chapter was somewhat contrived, the purpose was very important: showing how to interact with other layers of your application. Be it a data access layer, a business logic layer, a service layer, or anything else you might encounter in the real world, knowing how to fit it into your Stripes application is imperative. Just as important as interacting with other tiers of your application is learning to manage interaction between multiple ActionBeans. That is precisely what we will cover next.

CHAPTER 8

Interaction Between ActionBeans

This chapter will show how to put together what we've learned, by creating a simple application consisting of multiple pages and multiple ActionBeans. Our application will contain the following: `LoginActionBean`, which will be used to authenticate users; `ApplicationMenuActionBean`, which displays a menu to the user; and `Page1ActionBean` and `Page2ActionBean`, which are accessible from our menu. We also have a `UserDAO` object, which is a mock Data Access Object used to look up and authenticate usernames and passwords.

Login

We will start with the most complex of these objects, `LoginActionBean` (see Listing 8-1).

Listing 8-1. LoginActionBean.java

```
public class LoginActionBean extends BaseActionBean {

    private String username;
    private String password;
    private String status;

    @DefaultHandler
    public Resolution index(){
        return new ForwardResolution("/jsp/chapter8/login.jsp");
    }

    @HandlesEvent("login")
    public Resolution login(){
      UserDAO userDAO = new UserDAO();
      boolean loginSuccess = userDAO.login(username, password);

      Resolution resolution = null;
      if(loginSuccess){
        resolution = new RedirectReso
      } else {
        status = "Login failed";
        resolution = this.index();
      }
      return resolution;
    }

   // Getters and Setters...
}
```

The default action will be to display a login screen.

UserDAO is used to see if the username and password are correct.

If the login was successful we redirect to the Menu.

If login fails, we run index() and return its Resolution. An alternative would be to redirect to LoginActionBean, though by using this method we can set 'status' to "Login failed".

Brent Watson, *Stripes by Example*, DOI 10.1007/978-1-4842-0980-6_8

EXPERT TIP

The login mechanism in this application is not robust or secure. Ideally, all method calls would confirm that the user is logged in before allowing the method to execute. This is possible using servlet filters or by configuring Stripes interceptors, which allow you to define hooks in your application and provide custom code to run at various stages in the Stripes ActionBean life cycle. We will cover interceptors in Chapter 13.

Listing 8-2 shows the login form that uses the ActionBean from Listing 8-1.

Listing 8-2. login.jsp

```
<%@ taglib prefix="c" uri="http://java.sun.com/jsp/jstl/core" %>
<%@ taglib prefix="stripes"
        uri="http://stripes.sourceforge.net/stripes.tld"%>

<html>
    <body>
        <h1>Login:</h1>                          Display status message if it is set.
        <c:if test="${actionBean.status!=null}">
            <b>${actionBean.status}</b><br /><br />
        </c:if>

        <stripes:form beanclass="org.stripesbook.chapter8.LoginActionBean">
            Username: <stripes:text name="username" /><br />
            Password: <stripes:text name="password" /><br />
            <stripes:submit name="login" value="OK" />
        </stripes:form>
        <i>Hint: "user"/"pass"</i>
    </body>
</html>
```

This form looks like the one shown in Figure 8-1.

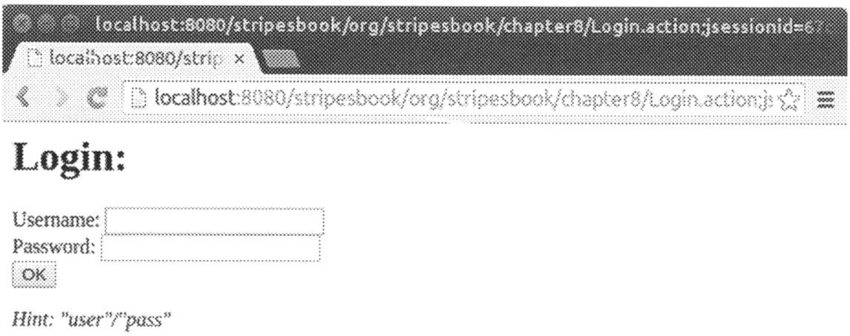

Figure 8-1. *Login form defined in login.jsp*

Instead of worrying about more database code, we will mock our UserDAO with hardcoded username and password values ("user" and "pass"), as shown in Listing 8-3.

Listing 8-3. UserDAO.java

```
public class UserDAO {
    public static String VALID_USERNAME = "user";
    public static String VALID_PASSWORD = "pass";

    /**
     * Would usually be a DB select statement
     */
    public boolean login(String username, String password){
        if(VALID_USERNAME.equals(username) &&
           VALID_PASSWORD.equals(password)){
            return true;
        } else{
            return false;
        }
    }
}
```

Providing something other than "user" / "pass" will result in seeing the login screen again, along with a "Login failed" message at the top of the page. Providing the correct credentials will forward us to ApplicationMenuActionBean, which simply displays a menu of other pages to visit.

Application Pages

The remainder of the application is composed of three pages that provide navigability between each other. These will be a menu page, a "page 1", and a "page 2". Interaction between the menu and page 2 is important in that it shows how parameters can be passed to an ActionBean in a URL instead of having to use a form. As you will see, this is done using the <stripes:param> tag within a <stripes:link> tag. First, let us review Listings 8-4 and 8-5, which define the ActionBean used to display the menu page and the corresponding JSP page, respectively.

Listing 8-4. ApplicationMenuActionBean.java

```
public class ApplicationMenuActionBean extends BaseActionBean {

    @DefaultHandler
    public Resolution index(){
        return new ForwardResolution("/jsp/chapter8/application_menu.jsp");
    }

}
```

Listing 8-5. application_menu.jsp

```
<%@ taglib prefix="stripes"
           uri="http://stripes.sourceforge.net/stripes.tld"%>

<html>
  <body>
    <h1>Menu:</h1>
    <ul>
     <li>
      <stripes:link beanclass="org.stripesbook.chapter8.Page1ActionBean">
         Page 1
      </stripes:link>
     </li>
     <li>
       <stripes:link beanclass="org.stripesbook.chapter8.Page2ActionBean">
          <stripes:param name="someParam">Passed in Value</stripes:param>
           Page 2 <i>(with a URL parameter).</i>
        </stripes:link>
      </li>
      <li>
        <stripes:link beanclass="org.stripesbook.chapter8.LoginActionBean">
           Back to login
        </stripes:link>
      </li>
    </ul>

  </body>
</html>
```

This is new; <stripes:param> lets us pass parameter values into an ActionBean via a link. This is accomplished by URL GET parameters being set.
Eg: http://.../action/page2**?someParam=Passed+in+Value**

Page1ActionBean and Page2ActionBean will simply contain links to the other available pages. By this point, you should be able to guess what Page1ActionBean, Page2ActionBean, and their corresponding JSP files look like. See if you can visualize what these look like and then read on to see if you are correct, starting with the first page (see Listings 8-6 and 8-7).

Listing 8-6. Page1ActionBean.java

```
public class Page1ActionBean extends BaseActionBean{

    @DefaultHandler
    public Resolution index(){
        return new ForwardResolution("/jsp/chapter8/page1.jsp");
    }

}
```

Listing 8-7. page1.jsp

```
<%@ taglib prefix="stripes"
        uri="http://stripes.sourceforge.net/stripes.tld"%>

<html>
  <body>
    <h1>Page 1</h1>
    <ul>
     <li>
         <stripes:link beanclass="org.stripesbook.chapter8.
ApplicationMenuActionBean">
          Back to Menu
         </stripes:link>
     </li>
     <li>
         <stripes:link beanclass="org.stripesbook.chapter8.LoginActionBean">
          Back to login
         </stripes:link>
      </li>
    </ul>
  </body>
</html>
```

EXPERT TIP

You are able to navigate between JSP pages without an ActionBean. This is done by linking directly the to a JSP file. For example:

```
<stripes:link href="${pageContext.request.contextPath}/jsp/chapter8/
page1.jsp">
   Direct jsp link
</stripes:link>
```

This works provided that the target JSP file does not try to reference any ActionBean variables via `${actionBean}`, since no ActionBean will be in scope. When doing this, Stripes does in fact support some of its features, such as interceptors and references to various Stripes properties, which we will see in Chapters 12 and 13. This is because `*.jsp` calls are configured to go through the `StripesFilter` (see Chapter 2).

The code for the second page is shown in Listings 8-8 and 8-9.

Listing 8-8. Page2ActionBean.java

```
public class Page2ActionBean extends BaseActionBean {
    private String someParam;

    @DefaultHandler
    public Resolution index(){
        return new ForwardResolution("/jsp/chapter8/page2.jsp");
    }

    public String getSomeParam() {
        return someParam;
    }

    public void setSomeParam(String someParam) {
        this.someParam = someParam;
    }
}
```

Listing 8-9. page2.jsp

```
<%@ taglib prefix="stripes"
           uri="http://stripes.sourceforge.net/stripes.tld"%>
<html>
  <body>
    <h1>Page 2</h1>
    <b>Passed In Parameter</b>: ${actionBean.someParam}

    <ul>
     <li>
         <stripes:link
              beanclass="org.stripesbook.chapter8.
ApplicationMenuActionBean">
           Back to Menu
         </stripes:link>
     </li>
     <li>
         <stripes:link beanclass="org.stripesbook.chapter8.LoginActionBean">
           Back to login
         </stripes:link>
     </li>
    </ul>
  </body>
</html>
```

Here is our new application in its entirety, starting with the form that we saw in Figure 8-1, which allows us to enter the username and password that will be submitted to `LoginActionBean`'s `login()` method (see Listing 8-1). Figure 8-2 shows a user entering their username and password.

localhost:8080/stripesbook/org/stripesbook/chapter8/Login.action;jsessionid=67

localhost:8080/strip ×

localhost:8080/stripesbook/org/stripesbook/chapter8/Login.action;j

Login:

Username: user
Password: pass
OK

Hint: "user"/"pass"

Figure 8-2. *Filled-in login form*

Upon submitting this form, one of two things will happen—depending on if the username and password are entered correctly or not. If authentication fails, the user will be redirected back to the login screen with a "Login failed" message displayed (see Listing 8-1 and Listing 8-2). If the login is successful, the user will be presented with what we see in Figure 8-3, which is the output from Listings 8-4 (`ApplicationMenuActionBean`) and 8.- (`application_menu.jsp`).

Menu:

- Page 1
- Page 2 *(with a URL parameter)*.
- Back to login

Figure 8-3. *Menu page as defined in application_menu.jsp, providing links to the next two pages*

This menu page presents the user with three links. The first link will execute the code in Listing 8-6 (`Page1ActionBean`). The resultant page is shown in Figure 8-4.

Page 1

- Back to Menu
- Back to login

Figure 8-4. *First page linked to from application_menu.jsp*

The second link will execute the code in Listing 8-8 (`Page2ActionBean`), which also shows how we can pass data via the URL as opposed to via POST parameters, as we have done so far. Figure 8-5 shows this page.

- Back to Menu
- Back to login

Figure 8-5. *Second page linked to from application_menu.jsp, showing how parameters can be passed via the URL*

The important item to note about our second page is the format of the URL, `http://localhost:8080/stripesbook/org/stripesbook/chapter8/Page2.action?someParam=Passed+in+Value`. As you can see, we have passed a parameter using a standard HTTP GET value using the syntax `?someParam=Passed+in+Value`. In Listing 8-8, we see that this mapped to a standard class variable, `someParam`.

Review

Over the span of the past six chapters, we have seen configuration and setup code, JSP code, database code, and, of course, ActionBeans—including interaction between them. To summarize this chapter, JSP-to-ActionBean-to-JSP interaction is usually accomplished by displaying a web page containing links and/or forms that submit to other ActionBeans, which take the input required to do some computation or processing, and then display another JSP web page to the user. Wash, rinse, repeat.

With these tools in hand, you have the pieces necessary to build a fully functionally web application. We will now explore an important feature that could be used to enhance such an application: data validation.

CHAPTER 9

Validation

Data validation is a major headache for most web developers. Data must be validated for a number of potential problems before it can be used, such as checking for data that is blank/empty when it should not be (e.g., username fields), improperly formatted fields (e.g., phone numbers), invalid data types (e.g., age must be numeric), invalid lengths (e.g., password must be greater than six characters), and the list goes on.

Luckily, Stripes provides a very nice validation mechanism built into ActionBeans and exposed through field-level annotations. These are `@Validate` and `@ValidateNestedProperties`, and `@DontValidate`.

`@Validate` is used to perform validation on your local variables in your ActionBeans. `@ValidateNestedProperties` can be used to perform validation of nested data types, such as our `DvdDTO` object from Chapter 6. Both are powerful and simple to use. `@DontValidate` is a method-level annotation that can be used to tell Stripes to skip validation checks on a certain method.

EXPERT TIP

Validation happens as a step in the ActionBean life cycle. It occurs at a stage called *BindingAndValidation*. In this step, data is converted to the proper type (since all input types from HTML forms are sent as text, Stripes converts the text to the proper Java type based on the data type of the field being set, such as `Date`, `String`, `int`, `Integer`, `Long`, `boolean`, etc.). This step in the life cycle occurs before your target method is executed. The various life cycle stages are discussed in more detail in Chapter 11.

Brent Watson, *Stripes by Example*, DOI 10.1007/978-1-4842-0980-6_9

@Validate Annotation

Listing 9-1 is an example of @Validate in action.

Listing 9-1. ValidationActionBean.java

```
    private String name;

    @Validate(required=true, minvalue=0, maxvalue=115)
    private int age;

    @Validate(required=false,
              mask="\\d{3}-\\d{3}-\\d{4}")
    private String phoneNumber;

    @DefaultHandler
    @DontValidate
    public Resolution index(){
        return new ForwardResolution("/jsp/chapter9/form.jsp");
    }

    @HandlesEvent("submit")
    public Resolution submit(){
        return new ForwardResolution("/jsp/chapter9/results.jsp");
    }

    // Getters and Setters... (No special annotations on getters or setters)
}
```

This is a regular expression used to check for a property formatted phone number. eg: 111-222-3333.

Don't run validation rules here because all fields will be blank

Other attributes are available on the @Validate annotation. Table 9-1 is a description of each taken from the Stripes Javadoc (`http://stripes.sourceforge.net/docs/current/javadoc/net/sourceforge/stripes/validation/Validate.html`).

Table 9-1. Table Caption

Attribute	Purpose
converter (A class that extends TypeConverter)	A type converter used to convert this field from String to its rich object type.
encrypted (boolean)	If true, then a parameter value to be bound to this field must be an encrypted string.
expression	Specifies an expression in the JSP expression language that should be evaluated to check the validity of this field.
field	The name of the field to validate.
ignore	If set to true, will cause the property to be ignore by binding and validation, even if it was somehow submitted in the request.
label	The natural language name to use for the field when reporting validation errors, generating form input labels, and so forth.
mask	Specifies a regular expression mask used to check the format of the String value submitted.
maxlength	Specifies a maximum length of characters that must be submitted.
maxvalue (double)	Specifies the maximum numeric value acceptable for a numeric field.
minlength	Specifies a minimum length of characters that must be submitted.
minvalue (double)	Specifies the minimum numeric value acceptable for a numeric field.
on (String[])	If required=true, restricts the set of events to which the required check is applied.
required (boolean)	If set to true, requires that a non-null, non-empty values must be submitted for the field.
trim	Trims whitespace from the beginning and end of request parameter values before attempting validation, type conversion, or binding.

That is all you need to add to your ActionBeans to add validation rules. To give friendly feedback messages to your users in the event of a validation error, you simply have to add (<stripes:errors />) to your JSP page. That's it. We're done.

Listing 9-2 is our example JSP.

Listing 9-2. form.jsp

```
<%@ taglib prefix="c" uri="http://java.sun.com/jsp/jstl/core" %>
<%@ taglib prefix="stripes"
           uri="http://stripes.sourceforge.net/stripes.tld"%>

<html>
    <body>
      <h1>Validation:</h1>
      <stripes:errors />

      <stripes:form beanclass="${actionBean.class}">
        Name: <stripes:text name="name" /><br />
        Age: <stripes:text name="age" /><br />
        Phone Number: <stripes:text name="phoneNumber" />(xxx-xxx-xxxx)<br
/>

      <stripes:submit name="submit" value="OK" />
      </stripes:form>

    </body>
</html>
```

A filled-in example of the form is shown in Figure 9-1.

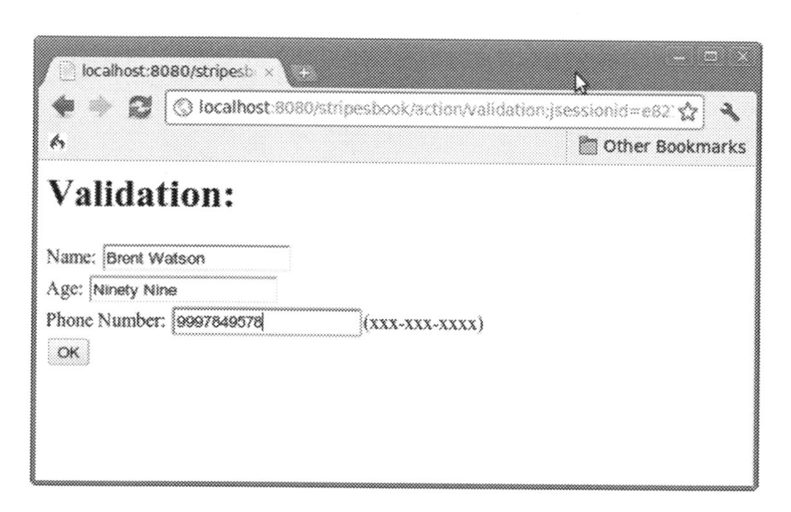

Figure 9-1. *Form with two invalid values*

The values in Figure 9-1 produce the results shown in Figure 9-2.

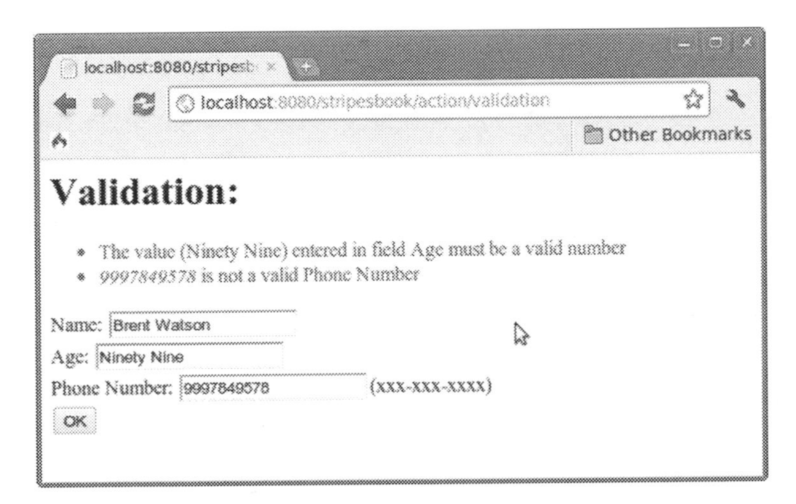

Figure 9-2. *Validation error messages*

If you don't like the format of the default validation output, you can override it using a few extra `<stripes:...>` tags, as shown in Listing 9-3.

Listing 9-3. form.jsp

```
<%@ taglib prefix="c" uri="http://java.sun.com/jsp/jstl/core" %>
<%@ taglib prefix="stripes"
        uri="http://stripes.sourceforge.net/stripes.tld"%>

<html>
    <body>
      <h1>Validation:</h1>
      <div class="errors">
        <stripes:errors>
          <stripes:errors-header>
            <b>Validation Errors</b><br />
          </stripes:errors-header>
          <stripes:individual-error/><br />
          <stripes:errors-footer><hr/></stripes:errors-footer>
        </stripes:errors>
      </div>

      <stripes:form beanclass="${actionBean.class}">
        Name: <stripes:text name="name" /><br />
        Age: <stripes:text name="age" /><br />
        Phone Number: <stripes:text name="phoneNumber" />(xxx-xxx-xxxx)<br />

      <stripes:submit name="submit" value="OK" />
      </stripes:form>

    </body>
</html>
```

We start with the bolded text validation errors.

Each individual error will be output, followed by a line break.

We end with a horizontal ruler.

As you can see in Figure 9-3, our markup has now changed.

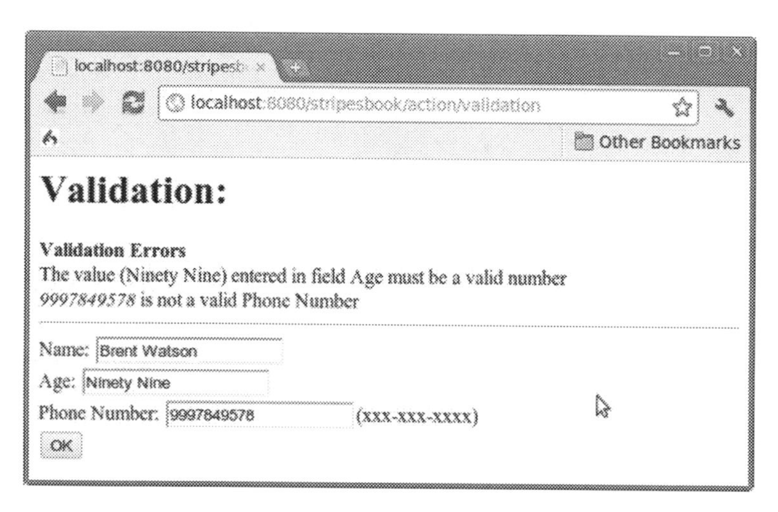

Figure 9-3. *Validation error messages with custom formatting applied*

@ValidateNestedProperties Annotation

We're not quite done yet. We have one validation annotation left: `@ValidateNestedProperties`. Again, this is used to validate nested values (as shown in Listing 9-4), usually contained in a DTO object, or something of the sort.

Listing 9-4. ValidationAdvancedActionBean.java

```
@UrlBinding("/action/advancedvalidation")
public class ValidationAdvancedActionBean extends BaseActionBean {

    @Validate(required=true) //default is false
    private String name;

    @ValidateNestedProperties({
     @Validate(field="address1", required=true, minlength=10, maxlength=100),
     @Validate(field="city", required=true, minlength=3, maxlength=20),
     @Validate(field="state", required=true, minlength=4, maxlength=20),
     @Validate(field="country", required=true, minlength=4, maxlength=30),
     @Validate(field="zipCode", required=true,
              minlength=5, maxlength=7)  //5 for zips, 7 for postal codes
    })
```

```
    private AddressDTO address;
    @DefaultHandler
    @DontValidate //don't run validation rules here
    public Resolution index(){
        return new ForwardResolution("/jsp/chapter9/advanced/form.jsp");
    }

    @HandlesEvent("submit")
    public Resolution submit(){
        return new ForwardResolution("/jsp/chapter9/advanced/results.jsp");
    }

    // Getters and Setters...
```

The preceding annotations can be used to validate an AddressDTO object, defined in Listing 9-5.

Listing 9-5. AddressDTO.java

```
public class AddressDTO {

    private String address1;
    private String address2;
    private String city;
    private String state;
    private String country;
    private String zipCode;

    // Getters and Setters...
}
```

Listing 9-5 can be tested by making some data entry errors, as shown in Figure 9-4.

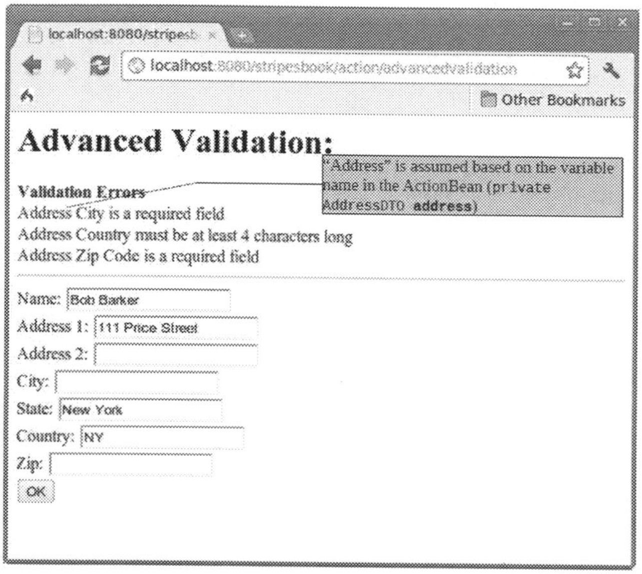

Figure 9-4. Validation errors from nested object properties

Review

Stripes makes validation easy. With three simple annotations—`@Validate`, `@ValidateNestedProperties`, and `@DontValidate`—you can have an application that guaranties safe and sanitized input values.

CHAPTER 10

Resolutions

So far we've seen two of Stripes resolutions: `ForwardResolution`, which is used to specify the JSP that will be run, and `RedirectResolution`, which is used to perform an HTTP redirect. Though Stripes actually has seven classes that implement the `Resolution` interface, only a few are commonly used. This chapter will explain some advanced features of `RedirectResolution` and extend our knowledge to include two additional resolutions: `StreamingResolution`, which is used to stream data back to the client (such as text or file data), and `ErrorResolution`, which takes an error number (e.g., 404) and a message to send back to the client.

Starting the Resolution Examples

Let's begin by setting up an ActionBean containing what we've seen before, and then improve upon it (see Listing 10-1).

Listing 10-1. OtherResolutionsActionBean.java — Version 1

```
@UrlBinding("/action/otherresolutions")
public class OtherResolutionsActionBean extends BaseActionBean {

    private static String message;

    @DefaultHandler
    @HandlesEvent("forwardresolution")
    public Resolution forwardResolution() {
        return new ForwardResolution("/jsp/chapter10/resolutions.jsp");
    }

    @HandlesEvent("simpleredirectresolution")
    public Resolution simpleRedirectResolution() {
        message = "Simple RedirectResolution was executed";
        return new RedirectResolution(OtherResolutionsActionBean.class);
    }

    // Getters and Setters...
}
```

Be very careful when using static fields. Values will be shared between requests & users.

We've seen this before.

We've seen this as well; it will redirect and end up running @DefaultHandler.

Brent Watson, *Stripes by Example*, DOI 10.1007/978-1-4842-0980-6_10

RedirectResolution

RedirectResolution contains many methods that can be used to mold the request, depending on your needs. These methods are shown in Table 10-1.

Table 10-1. *Caption*

Method	Use	Example
addParameter (String, String)	Adds variable(s) to the redirect URL as GET parameters. These values will be set in the target ActionBean (provided there are the appropriate setter methods).	addParameter ("someParam", "myValue");
IncludeRequestParameters (boolean)	All existing field values in the current ActionBean will be included as parameters on the redirect.	includeRequestParameters (true)
setPermanent(boolean)	Returns a 301 (Permanent move, which browsers will remember), instead of a 302 (temporary move).	setPermanent(true)
RedirectResolution (ActionBean, event)	This is a second constructor that can be used to specify which event will be executed. If left out, @DefaultEvent will be run.	RedirectResolution (OtherResolutionsActionBean.class, "forwardresolution");
RedirectResolution (String url)	This can be used to redirect to a specific URL instead of another ActionBean.	RedirectResolution ("http://.../action/someaction");

The preceding methods return 'this', allowing methods to be chained together, for example:

```
addParam("name1", "val1").addParam("name2", "val2").addParam("nameX", "valX");
```

Let's add some code to our ActionBean to see these methods in action. We will also put together a simple JSP page that triggers each option based on input parameters (Figure 10-1 shows how it will look). The ActionBean will check the input parameters and execute the proper code accordingly.

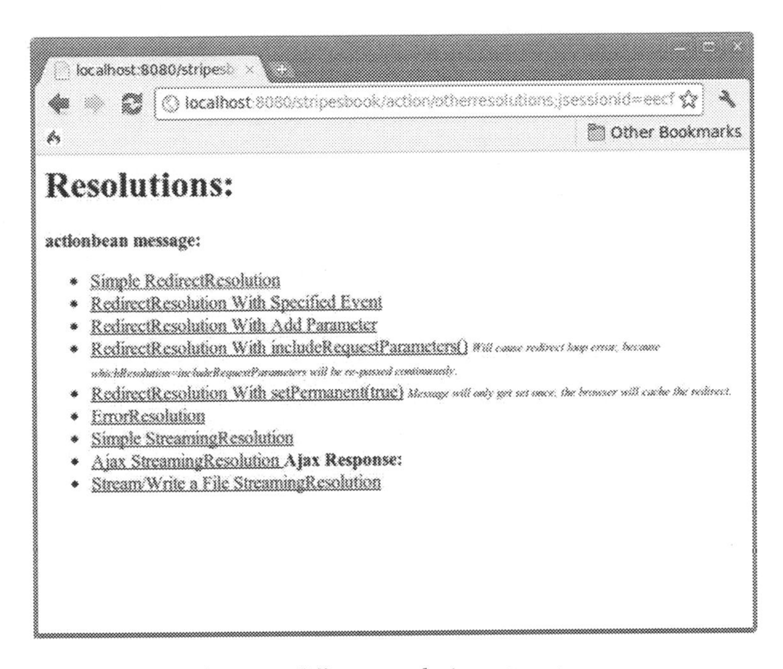

Figure 10-1. *Links to test different resolution return types*

Listing 10-2 contains the code for our JSP page.

Listing 10-2. resolutions.jsp

```
<%@ taglib prefix="c" uri="http://java.sun.com/jsp/jstl/core" %>
<%@ taglib prefix="stripes"
        uri="http://stripes.sourceforge.net/stripes.tld"%>

<html>

    <head>
      <script type="text/javascript"
      src="https://ajax.googleapis.com/ajax/libs/jquery/1.5.2/jquery.min.js">
      </script>
    </head>
    <body>
        <h1>Resolutions:</h1>
        <c:if test="${actionBean.message!=''}">
            <b>actionbean message:</b> <i>${actionBean.message}</i>
        </c:if>
        <ul>
            <li>
                <stripes:link beanclass="${actionBean.class}"
                              event="simpleredirectresolution">
                    Simple RedirectResolution
                </stripes:link>
            </li>
            <li>
                <stripes:link beanclass="${actionBean.class}"
                              event="complexredirectresolution">
                   <stripes:param name="whichResolution" value="withEvent" />
                        RedirectResolution With Specified Event
                </stripes:link>
            </li>
            <li>
               <stripes:link beanclass="${actionBean.class}"
                             event="complexredirectresolution">
                <stripes:param name="whichResolution" value="addParameter" />
                  RedirectResolution With Add Parameter
               </stripes:link>
            </li>
            <li>
               <stripes:link beanclass="${actionBean.class}"
                             event="complexredirectresolution">
                   <stripes:param name="whichResolution"
                                  value="includeRequestParameters" />
                      RedirectResolution With includeRequestParameters()
               </stripes:link>
               <i style="font-size: 8pt">Will cause redirect loop error,
because whichResolution=includeRequestParameters will be re-passed
continuously.</i>
            </li>
            <li>
              <stripes:link beanclass="${actionBean.class}"
                            event="complexredirectresolution">
                <stripes:param name="whichResolution" value="setPermanent" />
                    RedirectResolution With setPermanent(true)
              </stripes:link>
              <i style="font-size: 8pt">Message will only get set once, the
browser will cache the redirect.</i>
            </li>
            <li>
                <stripes:link beanclass="${actionBean.class}"
                              event="complexredirectresolution">
                   <stripes:param name="whichResolution"
                                  value="someInvalidResolution" />
                    ErrorResolution
```

```
                </stripes:link>
            </li>
            <li>
                <stripes:link beanclass="${actionBean.class}"
                              event="simplestreamingresolution">
                    Simple StreamingResolution
                </stripes:link>
            </li>
            <li>
                <a href="#" onclick="doAjaxCall()">
                    Ajax StreamingResolution
                </a>
                <b>Ajax Response: </b>
                <div id="ajaxReponse" style="display: inline"></div>
            </li>
            <li>
                <stripes:link beanclass="${actionBean.class}"
                              event="streamfilestreamingresolution">
                    Stream/Write a File StreamingResolution
                </stripes:link>
            </li>
        </ul>
        <script type="text/javascript">
            function doAjaxCall(){
                $('#ajaxReponse').load('$
{pageContext.request.contextPath}/action/otherresolutions/ajaxresponsestreami
ngresolution');
            }
        </script>
    </body>
</html>
```

> Don't worry about this Ajax code for now. It will be explained in the "Streaming Resolution" section.

The ActionBean will check the input parameters and execute the proper code accordingly (see Listing 10-3).

Listing 10-3. OtherResolutionsActionBean.java — Version 2

```
@UrlBinding("/action/otherresolutions")
public class OtherResolutionsActionBean extends BaseActionBean {

    private static String message;
    private String whichResolution = "";

    @DefaultHandler
    @HandlesEvent("forwardresolution")
    public Resolution forwardResolution() {
        return new ForwardResolution("/jsp/chapter10/resolutions.jsp");
    }

    @HandlesEvent("simpleredirectresolution")
    public Resolution simpleRedirectResolution() {
        message = "Simple RedirectResolution was executed";
        return new RedirectResolution(OtherResolutionsActionBean.class);
    }
```

```
    @HandlesEvent("complexredirectresolution")
    public Resolution complexRedirectResolution() {

        if ("withEvent".equals(whichResolution)) {
            message = "Specified Event was executed";
            return new RedirectResolution(OtherResolutionsActionBean.class,
                        "forwardresolution");   //(Class, event)

        } else if ("addParameter".equals(whichResolution)) {
            message = "Add Parameter was executed";
            return new RedirectResolution(OtherResolutionsActionBean.class)
              .addParameter("someParam", "myValue");
            //.addParameter("someParam2", "myValue"); //These can be chained

        } else if ("includeRequestParameters".equals(whichResolution)) {
            message = "includeRequestParameters was executed";
            return new RedirectResolution(OtherResolutionsActionBean.class)
                .includeRequestParameters(true); //Add all existing params
        } else if ("setPermanent".equals(whichResolution)) {
            message = "setPermanent(true) was executed";
            return new RedirectResolution(OtherResolutionsActionBean.class)
            .setPermanent(true); //Returns a 301 (Permanent move) vs 302

        } else {
            return new ErrorResolution(500,
                    "Invalid resolution String [" + whichResolution + "]");

        }

    }

    // Getters and Setters...
}
```

Did you notice that last else block at the bottom? That's everything you need to know about ErrorResolution in a nutshell.

ErrorResolution

Listing 10-4 contains a few more examples of ErrorResolution.

Listing 10-4. Error Resolutions

```
@HandlesEvent("error1")
public Resolution errorResolutionOne(){
    return new ErrorResolution(404, "Page not found");
}
```

```
@HandlesEvent("error2")
public Resolution errorResolutionTwo(){
    return new ErrorResolution(500, "Database connection failure");
}

@HandlesEvent("error3")
public Resolution errorResolutionThee(){
    return new ErrorResolution(503, "Website down for maintenance");
}
```

StreamingResolution

Next up is the last of the new resolutions that we will cover: `StreamingResolution`. This is the most complex resolution because it can be used for multiple things. We will cover three possible uses: streaming back text (HTML, XML, text, JSON, or anything else you wish), streaming back text used as an Ajax response, and lastly, streaming a file. All three are shown in Listing 10-5.

Listing 10-5. OtherResolutionsActionBean.java — Final Version

```
@UrlBinding("/action/otherresolutions")
public class OtherResolutionsActionBean extends BaseActionBean {

    private static String message;
    private String whichResolution = "";

    @DefaultHandler
    @HandlesEvent("forwardresolution")
    public Resolution forwardResolution() {
        return new ForwardResolution("/jsp/chapter10/resolutions.jsp");
    }

    @HandlesEvent("simpleredirectresolution")
    public Resolution simpleRedirectResolution() {
        message = "Simple RedirectResolution was executed";
        return new RedirectResolution(OtherResolutionsActionBean.class);
    }

    @HandlesEvent("complexredirectresolution")
    public Resolution complexRedirectResolution() {
        //Removed for brevity
        //...
    }

    @HandlesEvent("simplestreamingresolution")
    public Resolution simpleStreamingResolution(){
        String str = "Simple text";
        return new StreamingResolution("text", new StringReader(str));

    }

    @HandlesEvent("ajaxresponsestreamingresolution")
    public Resolution ajaxResponseStreamingResolution(){
        String str = "ajax response from server";
        return new StreamingResolution("text", new StringReader(str));
    }

    @HandlesEvent("streamfilestreamingresolution")
    public Resolution streamFileStreamingResolution(){
        return new StreamingResolution("text/plain") {
          @Override
          public void stream(HttpServletResponse response) throws Exception {
                response.getWriter().write("READ ME\n");
                response.getWriter().write("=======\n");
                response.getWriter().write("Some important info...\n");
          }
        }.setFilename("readme.txt");
    }

    // Getters and Setters...
}
```

The only difference between these 2 methods will be how they are called from the JSP.

Here we override the stream() method and write our own content. This could be from an existing file or from generated data, as in this example.

How these methods are called and what they produce is just as important as the ActionBean code itself. The bottom of Listing 10-2, `resolutions.jsp`, contained the code used to call these methods. Go and review that if needed. You will notice that we are using the jQuery JavaScript library to perform our Ajax calls. If you are not familiar with Ajax, it's simply JavaScript calling the server and receiving a response vs. the entire browser doing so. If you are not familiar with jQuery, it provides many convenient methods for working with JavaScript, one of which is `load()`, which performs an Ajax call to a given URL and places the response in a specified area—in our example, the `div` with `id ajaxResponse`. Again, go review Listing 10-2 if you need to.

Let's see these three `StreamingResolutions` in action, starting with the plain text stream, as shown in Figure 10-2.

Figure 10-2. *Text output from a StreamingResolution object*

Next is the Ajax call (see Figure 10-3).

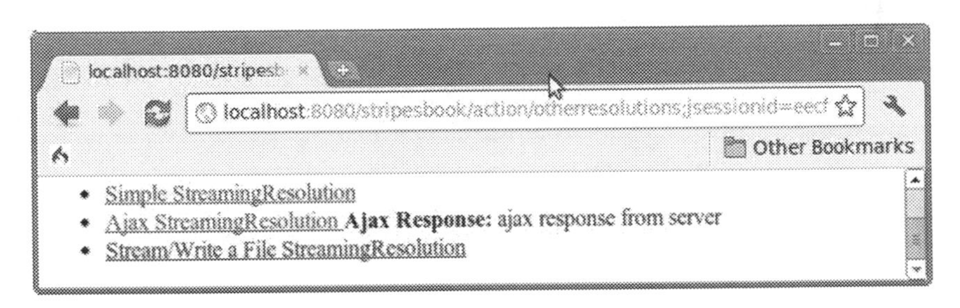

Figure 10-3. *Ajax response example from a StreamingResolution*

Finally, we have the file stream (see Figure 10-4).

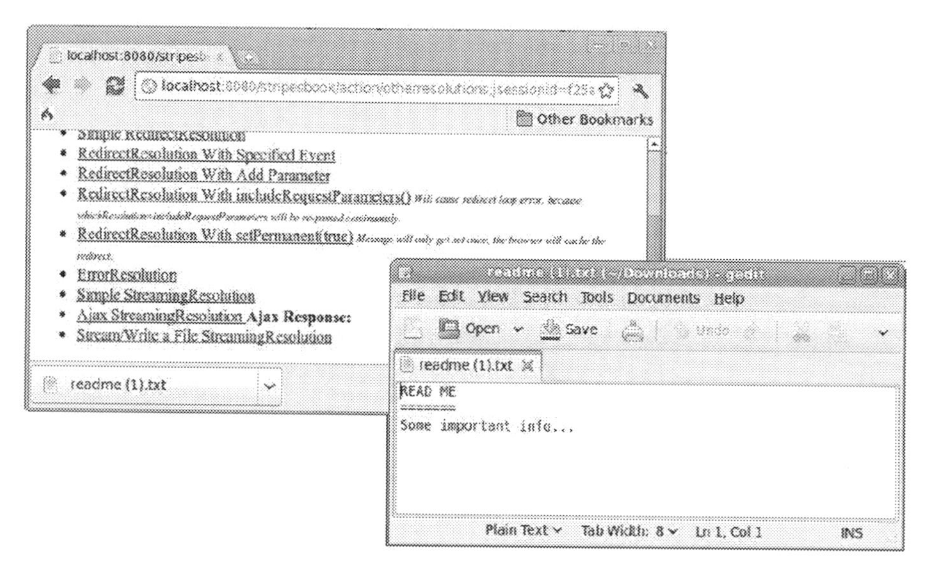

Figure 10-4. *File streamed for download using a StreamingResolution object*

Review

Redirects, HTTP errors, and data-streams—what more could you ask for? Well, Stripes does ship with a few more resolutions in case you find yourself in need. The exhaustive list includes `ErrorResolution`, `ForwardResolution`, `JavaScriptResolution`, `OnwardResolution`, `RedirectResolution`, `StreamingResolution`, and `ValidationErrorReportResolution`, though you can implement `Resolution` yourself if need be.

CHAPTER 11

Other Annotations

Stripes had the advantage of being built after Java 1.5 was released. This means that, unlike many other frameworks that rely heavily on XML configuration files (yuck!), the author (Tim Fennell) was able to take advantage of annotations. Stripes prides itself in the no-configuration stance it takes, and rightly so. This chapter covers the remainder of the annotations available in the Stripes framework.

We've seen most of the annotations in action already, such as `@UrlBinding`, `@DefaultHandler`, `@HandlesEvent`, and the validation annotations. This leaves us with the following left to explore: `@Before`, `@After`, `@SessionScope`, and `@SpringBean`. As you will see, these all do what you expect they would.

@SessionScope Annotation

A single instance of the class shown in Listing 11-1 will remain in the user's session vs. a new instance being made on every request.

Listing 11-1. AnnotationsActionBean.java — Version 1

```
@UrlBinding("/action/annotations")
@SessionScope
public class AnnotationsActionBean extends BaseActionBean  {

    // ActionBean method...
}
```

A single instance of this class will remain in the user's session vs. a new instance being made on every request.

A single instance of this class will remain in the user's session vs. a new instance being made on every request.

Brent Watson, *Stripes by Example*, DOI 10.1007/978-1-4842-0980-6_11

EXPERT TIP

Keeping an ActionBean object and all of its variables in session can be useful, but can also take up more memory than actually needed. An alternative, with a smaller memory footprint, is to store values in the user's session via the `HttpRequest` object:

```
getContext().getRequest().getSession().setAttribute("isLoggedIn",
"true");
```

With this in mind, you just might find that you don't need to use `@SessionScope`.

@Before and @After Annotations

Next up, `@Before` and `@After`. If you are familiar with unit testing, these annotations work the same as `@Before` and `@After` available with JUnit. Simply stated, if put on a method, that method will execute before (or after) your target method runs, as shown in Listing 11-2.

Listing 11-2. AnnotationsActionBean.java — Version 2

```
@UrlBinding("/action/annotations")
@SessionScope
public class AnnotationsActionBean extends BaseActionBean{

    private static int numRequests = 0;  //Works because of @SessionScope

    @Before
    public void before(){
        System.out.println("This will run before any event method runs.");
        numRequests++;
    }

    @After
    public void after(){
        System.out.println("This will run after the event method runs.");
        System.out.println(this.getContext());
    }
}
```

Both of these annotations also accept an `on="method_name"` parameter, allowing your method to be executed only before (or after) a specific method in your Actionbean. For example:

```
@Before(on="index")
@After(on="logout")
```

Also available is the `stages` parameter. This allows your before/after method(s) to be run at a specific stage in the Stripes life cycle. The default stage, if not specified, is after validation occurs. This means that the ActionBean will be instantiated and your input variables will already be set by the time your before/after method executes. This also means that if validation fails, your methods will not be executed.

Here are some examples:

```
@After (stages= {LifecycleStage.RequestComplete})
@Before(stages= {LifecycleStage.CustomValidation,
LifecycleStage.EventHandling})
```

The following are the life cycle stages in Stripes (in the order they are executed):

- `LifecycleStage.RequestInit`
- `LifecycleStage.ActionBeanResolution`
- `LifecycleStage.HandlerResolution`
- `LifecycleStage.BindingAndValidation`
- `LifecycleStage.CustomValidation`
- `@Before` *and* `@After` *methods will execute at this point if no stages are specified.*
- `LifecycleStage.EventHandling`
- `LifecycleStage.ResolutionExecution`
- `LifecycleStage.RequestComplete`

Table 11-1 shows descriptions of each life cycle stage, directly from the Stripes Javadoc (`http://stripes.sourceforge.net/docs/current/javadoc/net/sourceforge/stripes/controller/LifecycleStage.html`).

Table 11-1. *Captadsion*

Life Cycle Stage	Description
`RequestInit`	Executed before any processing occurs on the request. No Stripes processing is associated with this stage. It is simply provided as a hook for interceptors.
`ActionBeanResolution`	The first major life cycle stage. Involves the location of the ActionBean class that is bound to the URL being requested, and usually also the creation of a new instance of that class.
`HandlerResolution`	The second major life cycle stage. Involves the determination of the event name in the request (if there is one) and the location of the method that handles the event.
`BindingAndValidation`	The third major life cycle stage. Involves the processing of all validations specified through `@Validate` annotations, as well as the type conversion of request parameters and their binding to the ActionBean.
`CustomValidation`	The fourth major life cycle stage. Involves the execution of any custom validation logic exposed by the ActionBean.
`EventHandling`	The fifth major life cycle stage. The actual execution of the event handler method. Only occurs when the prior stages have produced no persistent validation errors.
`ResolutionExecution`	The sixth major life cycle stage. Is executed any time a `Resolution` is executed, either as the outcome of an event handler, or because some other mechanism short-circuits processing by returning a `Resolution`.
`RequestComplete`	The final life cycle stage. Executes in the final block of the request, so it will always be called when a request terminates, regardless of any other conditions. This is only useful for cleaning up, because `Resolution` execution has already occurred.

EXPERT TIP

The only one of these stages that requires a bit of explanation is LifecycleStage.ResolutionExecution, since we have not yet discussed how Stripes works internally. As described earlier, this life cycle stage happens before a resolution being returned from a method is executed. But what does that mean, *executed*? Well, very simply: the Resolution interface contains one method definition:

```
public void execute(HttpServletRequest request,
HttpServletResponse response)
```

This execute() method is called by the Stripes framework on any resolution object returned from your ActionBean method. In the case of a ForwardResolution, the JSP at the given path is loaded. In the case of a RedirectResolution, execute() returns an http-redirect header back to the user. In the case of a StreamingResolution, the stream() method is called.

In this way, you could create your own resolution object if you ever need anything very specific, such as an XmlResolution, JsonResolution, or Mp3Resolution.

Now that we understand the available Stripes life cycle options, let's see them in use in the context of the @Before and @After annotations (see Listing 11-3).

Listing 11-3. AnnotationsActionBean.java — Version 3

```
@UrlBinding("/action/annotations")
@SessionScope
public class AnnotationsActionBean extends BaseActionBean{

    @Before(on="index")
    public void before(){
      System.out.println("This will run before the index() method runs.");
    }

    @After(stages= {LifecycleStage.CustomValidation,
                    LifecycleStage.EventHandling,
                    LifecycleStage.RequestComplete})
    public void after(){
        System.out.println("This will run after the listed lifecycle stages.");
    }
}
```

@SpringBean Annotation

Spring is another popular framework used by Java developers. Though Spring has branched out to cover many areas of development, Spring's claim to fame is its Inversion of Control (IoC) / Dependency Injection (DI) ability. By defining *beans* (references to classes and values) in XML, you can let Spring inject objects into your code, thus decreasing coupling between objects—a good design principle.

Stripes provides a *field-level* annotation, @SpringBean, that will pull in a Spring bean at runtime. Listing 11-4 clearly demonstrates this in action.

Listing 11-4. AnnotationsActionBean.java — Version 4

```
@UrlBinding("/action/annotations")
public class AnnotationsActionBean extends BaseActionBean  {

    @SpringBean("myDAOBean")
    private DAO myDAO;

    //...

    public DAO getMyDAO() {
        return myDAO;
    }

    public void setMyDAO(DAO myDAO) {
        this.myDAO = myDAO;
    }
}
```

Spring injection also requires setter methods.

To round out this example, Listing 11-5 shows a very simple Spring XML file. These files usually become much more complex, but a complete explanation of Spring is outside the scope of this book.

Listing 11-5. spring-context.xml

```
<?xml version="1.0" encoding="UTF-8"?>
<beans xmlns="http://www.springframework.org/schema/beans"
       xmlns:xsi="http://www.w3.org/2001/XMLSchema-instance"
       xmlns:aop="http://www.springframework.org/schema/aop"
       xsi:schemaLocation="http://www.springframework.org/schema/beans
          http://www.springframework.org/schema/beans/spring-beans-3.0.xsd">

  <bean id="myDAOBean" class="com.stripesbook.daos.myDaoImpl">
     <property name="connection">

        ...connection info...
     </property>
  </bean>
</beans>
```

We have one last step in order for this to work. We must tell Stripes where the preceding XML file is located. In doing so, each time Stripes loads an ActionBean containing `@SpringBean`, it will delegate creating and setting any such fields to the Spring framework. To accomplish this, add the XML in Listing 11-6 to your `web.xml` configuration file.

Listing 11-6. web.xml

```
<listener>
    <listener-class>
        org.springframework.web.context.ContextLoaderListener
    </listener-class>
</listener>
<context-param>
    <param-name>contextConfigLocation</param-name>
    <param-value>/WEB-INF/spring-context.xml</param-value>
</context-param>
```

Tell Stripes to use Spring.

Tell Stripes where our Spring XML file resides.

This can be placed anywhere in `web.xml`. It is not part of any other existing XML nodes.

Now that we have covered all of Stripes' basic functionality in detail, including resolutions, JSPs/tag libraries, validation, and annotations, we can take a look at some of the corners of the framework.

Review

This chapter rounded out the annotations we will cover in this book:

- `@SessionScope`: Used to store ActionBeans in session
- `@Before` and `@After`: Useful for performing preprocessing or postprocessing operations in your code
- `@SpringBean`: Provides a simple facility to integrate with the Spring framework

CHAPTER 12

Internationalization

Skip this chapter. Yes, you read that correctly. Don't read it. That is unless what you are currently working on requires support for multiple languages. If not, my recommendation is to come back if and when this information is needed. Internationalization is difficult and configuration-heavy. You are better off learning the content of this chapter when it's needed rather than learning it just to forget it.

Are you still here? OK, then let's proceed.

Internationalization in Stripes

Internationalization is the act of allowing an application to serve up different languages and locales (e.g., English and Spanish, or US English and Great Britain English). Internationalization is commonly shortened to i18n (i[18_other_characters]n). That convention will be used for the remainder of the chapter.

Stripes helps greatly when adding i18n abilities to an application. Firstly, it figures out the user's local, language, and character encoding preferences based on their web browser settings. You are saved from having to figure this out yourself.

Stripes also automatically loads different configuration files based on these i18n preferences. In order for it to do this for you, you are expected to follow a set naming convention for your files, as you will see shortly.

Internationalization Setup and Configuration

To begin, we must first add i18n information to our `web.xml` file, as shown in Listing 12-1. This is added to the existing Stripes `<filter>` section that is already defined.

Brent Watson, *Stripes by Example*, DOI 10.1007/978-1-4842-0980-6_12

Listing 12-1. web.xml

```
<filter>
        <display-name>Stripes Filter</display-name>
        <filter-name>StripesFilter</filter-name>
        <filter-class>
                net.sourceforge.stripes.controller.StripesFilter
        </filter-class>
        <init-param>
            <param-name>ActionResolver.Packages</param-name>
            <param-value>
                org.stripesbook.chapter1,

            org.stripesbook.chapter2,
            org.stripesbook.chapterX...
            org.stripesbook.chapter15
        </param-value>
    </init-param>
    <init-param>
        <param-name>LocalePicker.Locales</param-name>
        <param-value>en_US,en_GB,fr_CA</param-value>
    </init-param>
</filter>
```

US English, Great Britain English, Canadian French

The preceding configuration defines that our application will support three languages: US English, Great Britain English, and Canadian French. As mentioned, a user's locale can be changed/configured in their web browser settings. If an exact match cannot be found, the best possible match from the available list of locals in `web.xml` is picked.

Stripes ships with a file called `StripesResources.properties`—located in `stripes-xxx.jar`. This is the default properties file, which contains error messages, validation error messages, and input data conversion error messages—all in English.

You are able to create your own `StripesResources.properties` file (the recommended setup is to copy the default onto your classpath, such as in your root package, as shown in Figure 12-1).

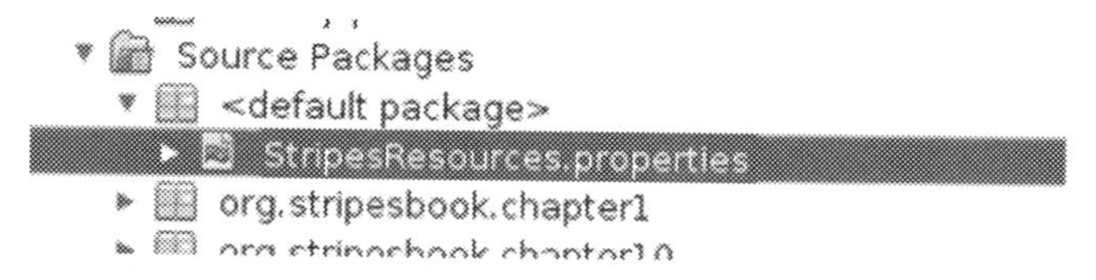

Figure 12-1. *Location of your StripesResources.properties file*

You can then add your own values to this file, as shown in Listing 12-2 (you will see how i18n fits into this setup soon).

Listing 12-2. StripesResources.properties

```
#
# STRIPES BY EXAMPLE VALUES
#
stripes.book.field.name=Field name from StripesResources.properties file

#
# STRIPES DEFAULT VALUES
#

# Resource strings used by the <stripes:errors> tag
stripes.errors.header=<ul>
stripes.errors.beforeError=<li style="text-decoration:none; color: #b72222;">
stripes.errors.afterError=</li>
stripes.errors.footer=</ul>
...
...
```

We can also use a full URI qualifier for the page from which this will be used.
"For example:"
/stripesbook/action/i18n.stripes.book.field.name=Field name from StripesResources.properties file

Using Internationalization Values

Now that we have our `StripesResources.properties` file in place, we can start to make use of it (and then extend it to allow for multiple languages). The values can be used in the view layer of our application through the use of `<stripes:...>` fields, shown in Listing 12-3.

Listing 12-3. i18n.jsp

```
<%@ taglib prefix="c" uri="http://java.sun.com/jsp/jstl/core" %>
<%@ taglib prefix="stripes"
           uri="http://stripes.sourceforge.net/stripes.tld"%>

<html>
    <body>
        <h1>Internationalization</h1>
        <stripes:label name="stripes.book.field.name" />
    </body>
</html>
```

This will look up the `stripes.book.field.name` key in our `StripesResources.properties` file, as shown in Figure 12-2.

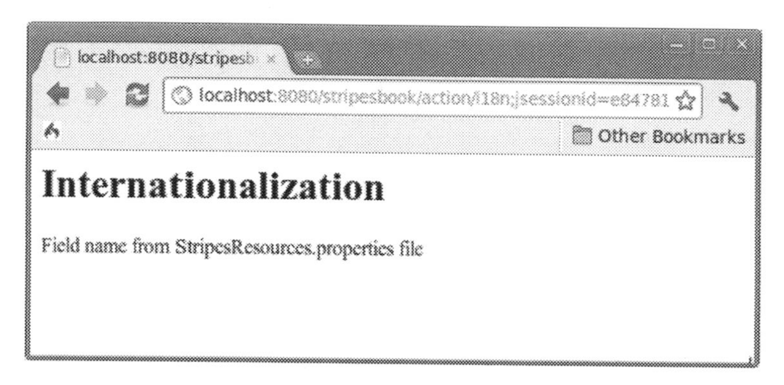

Figure 12-2. *Output from our internationalization field lookup*

Supporting Multiple Languages

Now, the key to i18n in Stripes: you create multiple `StripesResources.properties` files, ending with the local/location information.

For example, for our setup we would have the following files alongside the default `StripesResources.properties` file:

- English, US: `StripesResources_en_US.properties`
- English, Great Britain: `StripesResources_en_GB.properties`
- French, Canadian: `StripesResources_fr_CA.properties`

These files contain the required messages in the various languages our application is to support. For example, Listing 12-4 contains our `StripesResources_fr_CA.properties` file.

Listing 12-4. StripesResources_fr_CA.properties

```
#
# STRIPES BY EXAMPLE BOOK VALUES
#
stripes.book.field.name=Nom du champ du fichier StripesResources.properties

#
# STRIPES DEFAULT VALUES
#

# Resource strings used by the <stripes:errors> tag when there are no nested tags
stripes.errors.header=<ul>
stripes.errors.beforeError=<li style="text-decoration:none; color: #b72222;">

stripes.errors.afterError=</li>
stripes.errors.footer=</ul>
...
...
```

You can test this by changing your browser's language setting.

In Chrome, these settings are available under settings ➤ Preferences ➤ Under the hood ➤ Languages and Spell-checker Settings, as shown in Figure 12-3.

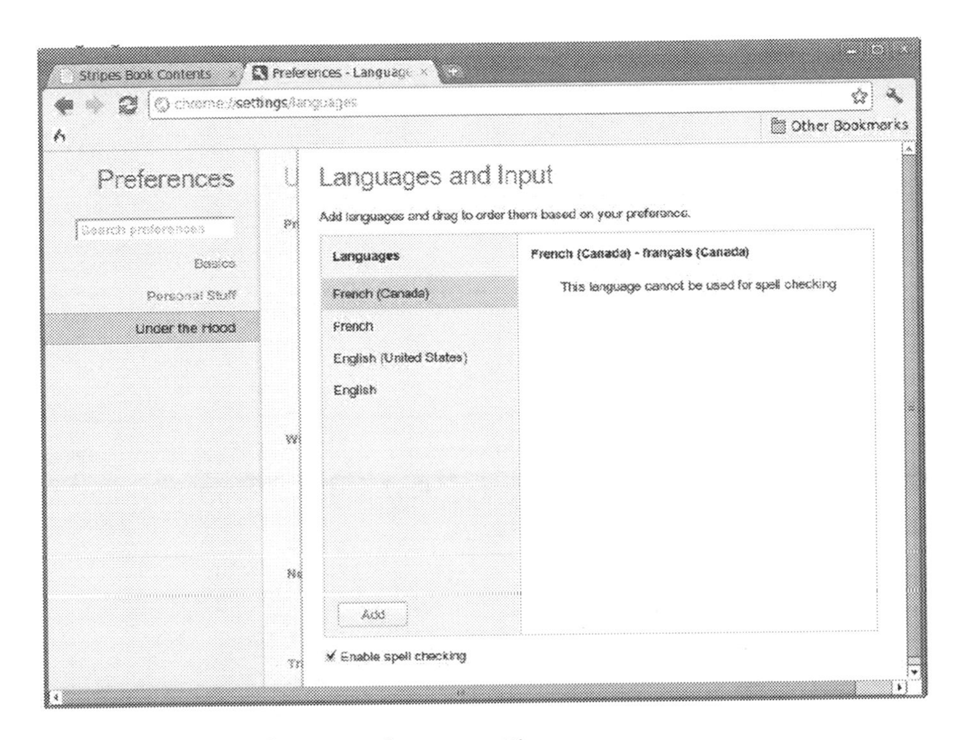

Figure 12-3. *How to change your language settings*

In Firefox this is available under Edit ➤ Preferences ➤ Content ➤ Languages ➤ Choose... And, in Internet Explorer it is available under Tools ➤ Internet Options ➤ General tab ➤ Languages.

Figure 12-4 shows the results of changing the language to French Canadian.

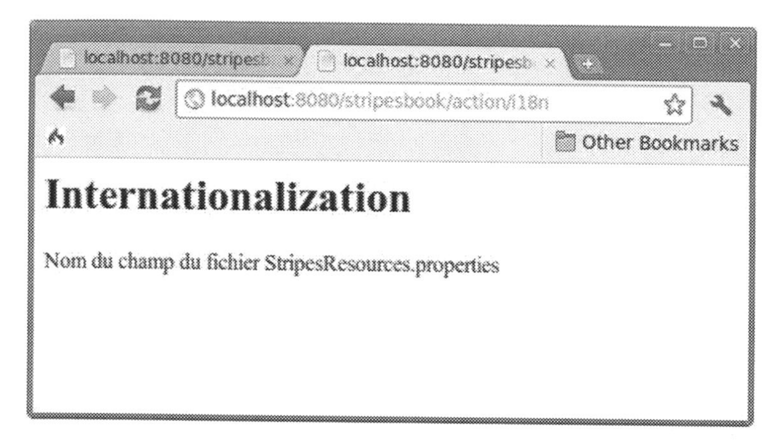

Figure 12-4. *Output from our internationalization field lookup after our language settings have been changed*

JSP Internationalization Value Lookups

Most of the Stripes form tags that output text contain the ability to look up their output values from the properties files. Listings 12-5 and 12-6 show some examples.

Listing 12-5. i18n_form.jsp

```
<%@ taglib prefix="c" uri="http://java.sun.com/jsp/jstl/core" %>
<%@ taglib prefix="stripes"
           uri="http://stripes.sourceforge.net/stripes.tld"%>

<html>
    <body>
        <h1>Internationalization Form Elements</h1>
        <stripes:form beanclass="${actionBean.class}">
            <stripes:label name="formdemo.label" /><br />
            <stripes:reset name="formdemo.reset" /><br />
            <stripes:button name="formdemo.button" /><br />
            <stripes:submit name="formdemo.submit" /><br />
        </stripes:form>
    </body>
</html>
```

Listing 12-6. StripesResources_xx_xx.properties

```
...
formdemo.label=My Label Value
formdemo.reset=My Reset Button Value

formdemo.button=My Button Value
formdemo.submit=My Submit Button Value
...
```

This is where using URL matching in your properties files can be a benefit. Since you do not want your field names to be too generic (e.g., `mylabel`) and you do not want the fields in the ActionBeans that you bind to to be too specialized (e.g., `localizationDemoPageNameLabel`), adding the URL path to your properties file values saves you from both of these issues (see Listings 12-7 and 12-8).

Listing 12-7. i18n_form.jsp — Version 2

```
<%@ taglib prefix="c" uri="http://java.sun.com/jsp/jstl/core" %>
<%@ taglib prefix="stripes"
        uri="http://stripes.sourceforge.net/stripes.tld"%>

<html>
    <body>
        <h1>Internationalization Form Elements</h1>
        <stripes:form action="/stripesbook/action/i18n">
            <stripes:label name="myLabel" /><br />
            <stripes:reset name="myReset" /><br />
            <stripes:button name="myButton" /><br />
            <stripes:submit name="mySubmit" /><br />
        </stripes:form>
    </body>
</html>
```

Action attribute URL is used in the property lookup.

Listing 12-8. StripesResources_xx_xx.properties — Version 2

```
...
/stripesbook/action/i18n.myLabel=My Label Value
/stripesbook/action/i18n.myReset=My Reset Button Value
/stripesbook/action/i18n.myButton=My Button Value
/stripesbook/action/i18n.mySubmit=My Submit Button Value
...
```

EXPERT TIP

The only oddity with using the preceding method to label fields is that they must be within a `<stripes:form>` tag that contains an `action=""` attribute. The `action` attribute is what Stripes matches on in the properties file. You can see this in effect in Listing 12-7.

A `beanclass` attribute on the form tag, though rendered as an action attribute in the HTML, will not work.

Though localization message lookups should happen in the view, the values can also be loaded from within an ActionBean if needed, though the facility to do this is slightly more involved:

```
String propertyValue = StripesFilter.getConfiguration()
        .getLocalizationBundleFactory().getFormFieldBundle(
            getContext().getLocale()).getString("your.property.name");
```

Stripes has many additional i18n options, including locale, language codes, script codes, and also character encoding. For more details, see the Java i18n documentation and the Stripes i18n documentation at the following sites:

- `http://download.oracle.com/javase/tutorial/i18n/locale/create.html`
- `https://stripesframework.atlassian.net/wiki/display/STRIPES/Localization`

Review

Though internationalization isn't the most exciting topic, Stripes at least makes it easy. By adding a few lines to `web.xml`, you suddenly get the ability to provide localized messages in your code. In the next chapter, you will learn about Stripes interceptors. *Echemos un vistazo* (let's take a look).

CHAPTER 13

Interceptors

Introduction to Interceptors

Stripes provides a facility to add hooks at various stages of your application. These are called Stripes *interceptors*. Interceptors are classes that implement Stripes' `Interceptor` interface and contain an `intercept()` method. Interceptors are a great way to do things like log requests or build security into an application.

Interceptors use the same `LifecycleStage` enums used by the `@Before` and `@After` annotations that we saw in Chapter 11. Refer back to Table 11-1 for details on each life cycle stage.

Let's jump right in (see Listing 13-1).

Listing 13-1. SimpleInterceptor.java

```
@Intercepts({LifecycleStage.ActionBeanResolution,
             LifecycleStage.HandlerResolution,
             LifecycleStage.BindingAndValidation,
             LifecycleStage.CustomValidation,
             LifecycleStage.EventHandling,
             LifecycleStage.ResolutionExecution})
public class SimpleInterceptor implements Interceptor{

    @Override
    public Resolution intercept(ExecutionContext context) throws Exception {
        //... your code ...
        return context.proceed();
    }
```

This interceptor will run at all of the listed LifeCycle stages.

If you are familiar with Java filters, you will notice the similarity. The `intercept()` method takes a context object, and at the end of your method, you must return `context.proceed()` in order for the application to proceed to the next step in the life cycle.

Interceptor Configuration

In order to "hook up" this code, we must now tell Stripes which package(s) our interceptors are in. This is done in `web.xml`, as shown in Listing 13-2.

Brent Watson, *Stripes by Example*, DOI 10.1007/978-1-4842-0980-6_13

Listing 13-2. web.xml

```
<filter>
    <display-name>Stripes Filter</display-name>
    <filter-name>StripesFilter</filter-name>
    <filter-class>
         net.sourceforge.stripes.controller.StripesFilter
    </filter-class>
    <init-param>
        <param-name>ActionResolver.Packages</param-name>
        <param-value>
            org.stripesbook.chapter1,
            org.stripesbook.chapter2,
            ...
            org.stripesbook.chapterX
        </param-value>
    </init-param>
    <init-param>
        <param-name>Extension.Packages</param-name>
        <param-value>org.stripesbook.chapter13</param-value>
    </init-param>
  </filter>
```

This package will be checked for any stripes extensions – including interceptors.

The ExecutionContext object passed into our intercept() function gives us a lot of information about the configuration and current execution context of the application—hence the name ExecutionContext.

Using Interceptor Data

Let's see what exactly we can do with our context object (see Listing 13-3).

Listing 13-3. SimpleInterceptor.java — Version 2

```
@Intercepts({LifecycleStage.ActionBeanResolution,
             LifecycleStage.HandlerResolution,
             LifecycleStage.BindingAndValidation,
             LifecycleStage.CustomValidation,
             LifecycleStage.EventHandling,
             LifecycleStage.ResolutionExecution})
public class SimpleInterceptor implements Interceptor{

    @Override
    public Resolution intercept(ExecutionContext context) throws Exception
{
        StringBuilder sb = new StringBuilder();
        sb.append("<b>Current ActionBean being requested: </b>");
        sb.append(context.getActionBean());
        sb.append("\n");
```

```
        sb.append("<b>Current ActionBean context: </b>");
        sb.append(context.getActionBeanContext());
        sb.append("\n");

        sb.append("<b>Method that will be called: </b>");
        sb.append(context.getHandler()); //Returns java.lang.reflect.Method.
                                           (Only available after
                                           HandlerResolution LifecycleStage)
        sb.append("\n");

        sb.append("<b>Current Lifecycle stage: </b>");
        sb.append(context.getLifecycleStage());
        sb.append("\n");

        sb.append("<b>Resolution: </b>");
        sb.append(context.getResolution());    //Resolution that will be
                                                 returned. (Only available
                                                 after ResolutionExecution
                                                 LifecycleStage)
        sb.append("\n\n");

        InterceptorDataActionBean.addInterceptorData(sb.toString());
        return context.proceed();
}
```

Listing 13-3. uses an InterceptorDataActionBean, on which we append new interceptor data. This will give us a utility to see the interceptor messages, though logging would be just as good. Listing 13-4 shows that ActionBean.

Listing 13-4. InterceptorDataActionBean.java

```
@UrlBinding("/action/interceptor")
public class InterceptorDataActionBean extends BaseActionBean {

    private static List<String> interceptorData = new ArrayList<String>();

    @DefaultHandler
    public Resolution index(){
        return new ForwardResolution("/jsp/chapter13/interceptordata.jsp");
    }

    public static void addInterceptorData(String data) {
        interceptorData.add(data);
    }

    public List<String> getInterceptorData() {
        return interceptorData;
    }

}
```

Using this, we can see our interceptor in action, as shown in Figure 13-1.

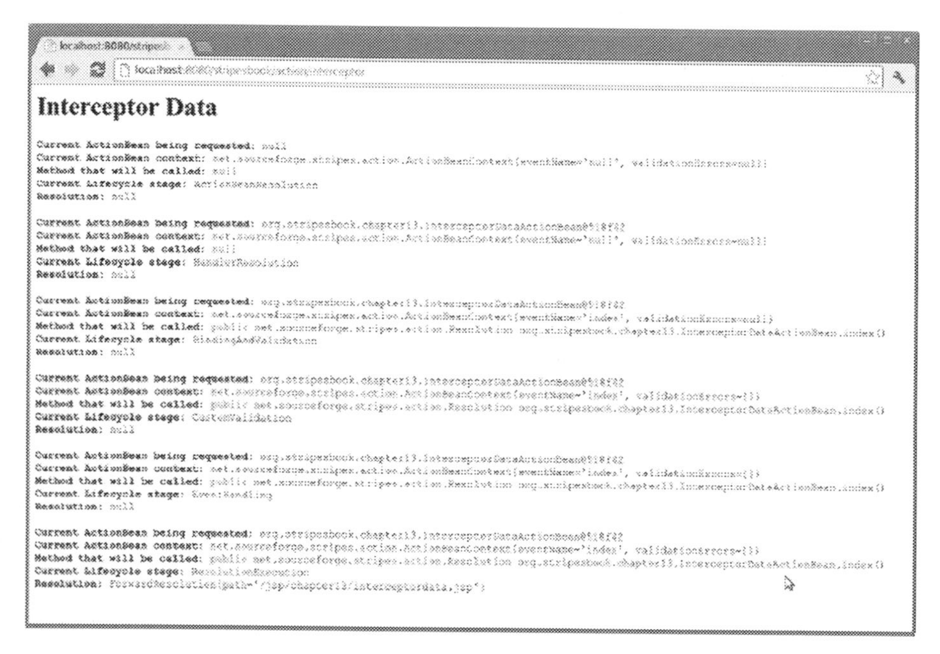

Figure 13-1. *Output from InterceptorDataActionBean for a simple GET request*

EXPERT TIP

Through `ExecutionContext` we are able to get to the user's `Session` object. This can be done with the following code:

```
context.getActionBeanContext().getRequest().getSession()
```

Using this, we can build various security interceptors that perform login (e.g., redirecting to a login screen if some `loggedIn` session variable is not yet set), perform role-based security, or even audit user actions.

Review

Interceptors can be very powerful. If you have logic that cuts through many parts of your code (such as execution timing or auditing), it can be easily integrated into your application using the tools discussed in this chapter.

CHAPTER 14

File Uploads

As with Chapter 12, I suggest you skip this chapter and come back to it only if you find yourself needing file upload capabilities in your application.

Note Before proceeding, either the Apache Commons FileUpload jar (`http://commons.apache.org/fileupload/`) or the COS jar (`www.servlets.com/cos/`) are needed to perform a file upload in Stripes. Add either one of these to your application as a jar file. Stripes is smart enough to use whichever one is available.

In addition, you need to create a local directory to which you can upload your files (e.g., `c:\myfileuploads`, or `/home/myuser/fileuploads`). Be sure this directory can be written to by whatever user is running your application server, otherwise you will receive errors when trying to upload files.

Uploading Files

Let's begin with an ActionBean that accepts a single file, as shown in Listing 14-1.

Brent Watson, *Stripes by Example*, DOI 10.1007/978-1-4842-0980-6_14

Listing 14-1. InterceptorDataActionBean.java

```
@UrlBinding("/action/fileupload")
public class FileUploadActionBean extends BaseActionBean {

    private FileBean fileToUpload;
    private String message;

    @DefaultHandler
    public Resolution index(){
        return new ForwardResolution("/jsp/chapter14/fileupload.jsp");
    }

    @HandlesEvent("upload")
    public Resolution upload() throws IOException{
        String saveToLocation = "c:\\myfiles\\" + fileToUpload.getFileName();
        fileToUpload.save(new File(saveToLocation));
        message = "File uploaded to " + saveToLocation;

        return this.index();
    }


    public FileBean getFileToUpload() {
        return fileToUpload;


}

public void setFileToUpload(FileBean fileToUpload) {
    this.fileToUpload = fileToUpload;
}

public String getMessage() {
    return message;
}

public void setMessage(String message) {
    this.message = message;
}
```

We can either save the file using the save() method, or we can process it using fileToUpload.getInputStream() and then remove it from temp space using fileToUpload.delete().

The JSP that allows for this upload uses a new tag, `<stripes:file>`, as shown in Listing 14-2.

Listing 14-2. fileupload.jsp

```
<%@ taglib prefix="c" uri="http://java.sun.com/jsp/jstl/core" %>
<%@ taglib prefix="stripes"
        uri="http://stripes.sourceforge.net/stripes.tld"%>

<html>
 <body>
  <h1>File Uploading</h1>

    <stripes:form
      action="${pageContext.request.contextPath}/action/fileupload/upload">

        <stripes:file name="fileToUpload" />
        <br /><br />
        <stripes:submit name="upload" value="Upload" />
    </stripes:form>

   ${actionBean.message}

 </body>
</html>
```

This is the third time we've seen `${pageContext...}` used. It returns the current contextRoot for our application (eg "/MyApplication").

When you click the Choose File button, this JSP page displays the Open File dialog box, as shown in Figure 14-1.

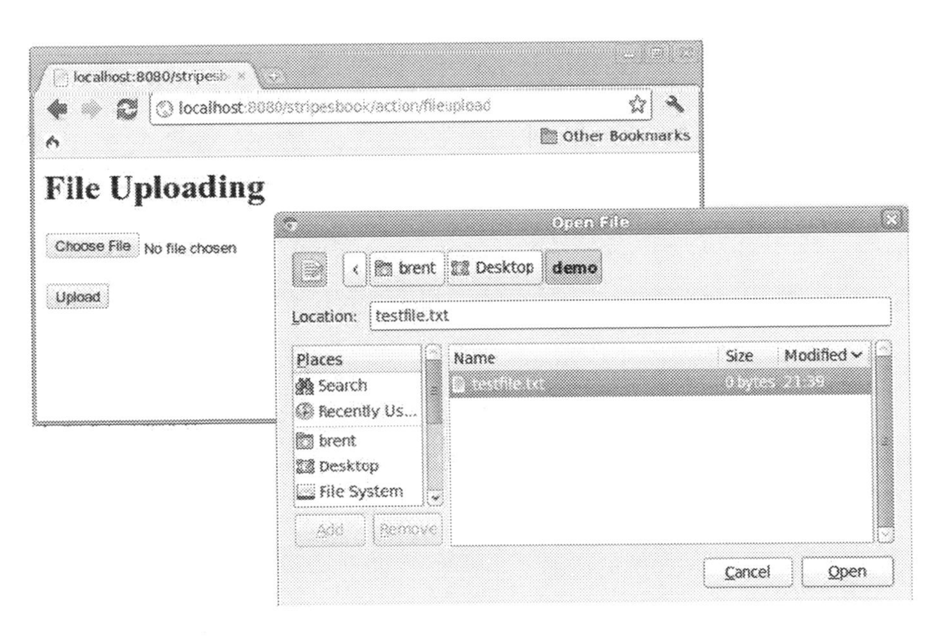

Figure 14-1. *Selecting a file to upload*

Uploading Multiple Files

Thankfully, Stripes makes multiple file uploads as easy as changing our `FileBean` property to a `List<FileBean>`, as shown in Listing 14-3.

Listing 14-3. MultipleFileUploadActionBean.java

```
@UrlBinding("/action/fileupload/multiple")
public class MultipleFileUploadActionBean extends BaseActionBean {

    private List<FileBean> filesToUpload;

    @DefaultHandler
    public Resolution index(){
        return new ForwardResolution("/jsp/chapter14/multiplefiles/"+
                                     "fileupload.jsp");
    }

    @HandlesEvent("multiupload")
    public Resolution upload() throws IOException{
        for (FileBean fileBean : filesToUpload) {
            if(fileBean!=null){

              String saveToLocation = "c:\\myfiles\\"+fileBean.getFileName();
              fileBean.save(new File(saveToLocation));
            }
        }
        return this.index();
    }

    public List<FileBean> getFilesToUpload() {
        return filesToUpload;
    }

    public void setFilesToUpload(List<FileBean> filesToUpload) {
        this.filesToUpload = filesToUpload;
    }

}
```

The file tags in the JSP can now be referenced using an index parameter, as shown in Listing 14-4.

Listing 14-4. fileupload.jsp

```
<%@ taglib prefix="c" uri="http://java.sun.com/jsp/jstl/core" %>
<%@ taglib prefix="stripes"
        uri="http://stripes.sourceforge.net/stripes.tld"%>


<html>
    <body>
        <h1>File Uploading</h1>
        <stripes:form beanclass="${actionBean.class}">
            File 1: <stripes:file name="filesToUpload[0]" /><br />
            File 2: <stripes:file name="filesToUpload[1]" /><br />
            File 3: <stripes:file name="filesToUpload[2]" /><br />
            <br />
            <stripes:submit name="multiupload" value="Upload" />
        </stripes:form>

        <c:if test="${actionBean.filesToUpload!=null}">
            Files uploaded:
            <ul>
               <c:forEach items="${actionBean.filesToUpload}" var="fileBean">
                    <li>${fileBean.fileName}</li>
               </c:forEach>
            </ul>
        </c:if>

    </body>
</html>
```

This will ouput file names after the upload is finished and the page is reloaded.

Figure 14-2 shows this code in action.

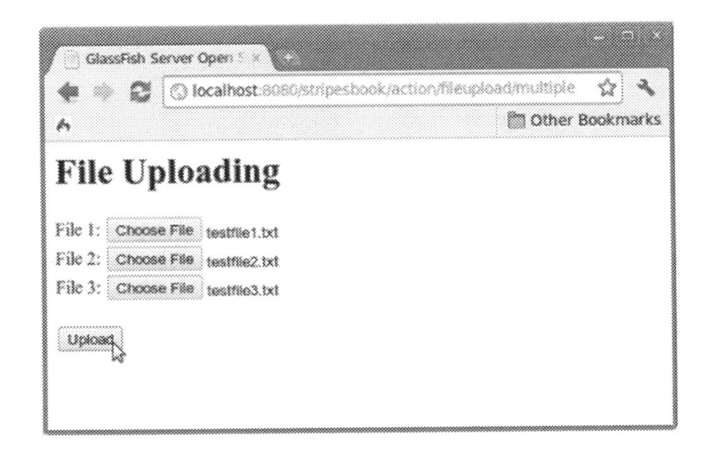

Figure 14-2. *Multiple files selected for upload*

After the files have finished uploading, the page will refresh and you will see a list of the uploaded files, as demonstrated in Figure 14-3.

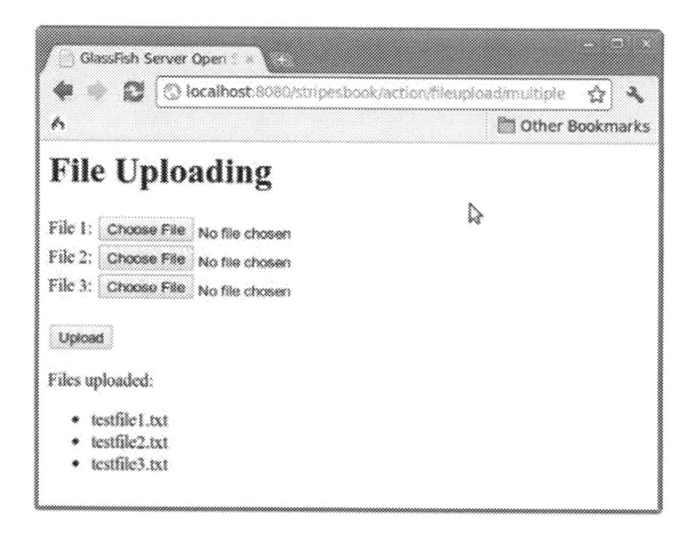

Figure 14-3. *Display after all files have been uploaded*

COS vs. Apache Commons FileUpload

Both the COS library and the Apache Commons FileUpload library are used in many companies' production systems. You can use either one without worry. So, why are there two options available instead of just one? COS was originally included with Stripes; however, its licensing requirements are stricter than that of the Apache Commons projects. COS was left in for backward compatibility and because the Apache Commons FileUpload causes another dependency—Apache Commons I.O. (`http://commons.apache.org/io/`), meaning that you need to have yet another jar file in your application (`commons-io.x.x.x.jar`). If you are building a sample application or an application that will be used only by you or your company, then either library is fine. If you plan on developing an application that will be shipped—along with the `cos.jar` file—to customers, then using the Apache Commons FileUpload option is your best choice.

EXPERT TIP

How does Stripes handle automatically selecting between the two file upload libraries without any configuration changes? Stripes first wraps each implementation with its own class, which implements a common interface. It then makes use of a special Java method, `Class.forName("your_classname")`, which attempts to initialize a class given the `String` equivalent of its full package and class name. If initializing the first class fails (because of import not being available!), it catches the error and tries to load the other option.

Review

If you need the ability to upload files in your application, the `FileBean` class is your friend. It manages the upload, save, and delete functions for you. An important thing to keep in mind is that `save()` moves the file from temp space to a specified folder; but if you do not plan on saving the files, be sure to use `delete()` to remove the temp file(s) once you are finished processing them.

CHAPTER 15

Good Design

After using a framework for a number of years, you come across good design practices. This chapter covers good design practice with Stripes.

Use BaseActionBean.java

First, use a base ActionBean. The `BaseActionBean.java` laid out in Chapter 3 (see Listing 3-4) and used throughout this book will help a lot. It will hide your `ActionBeanContext` get/set methods and also provide a place where you can include common methods, such as `getDatabaseFactory()` or `isUserLoggedIn()`. Keep in mind that such methods can be used by the JSPs too! For example, `${actionBean.userLoggedIn}`.

Use a base.jsp

The second suggestion is one that arguably could have been mentioned sooner—and that is using a base JSP file. Such a file can contain content-surrounding view code, such as HTML headers, JavaScript and CSS includes, a navigation bar, footers, and so forth. As usual, Stripes comes to our rescue by providing a simple facility by which to do this: `<stripes:layout-xxx>` tags (see Listings 15-1 and 15-2 for this in action).

Brent Watson, *Stripes by Example*, DOI 10.1007/978-1-4842-0980-6_15

Listing 15-1. base.jsp

```
<%@include file="taglibs.jsp" %>

<stripes:layout-definition>

    <html>
        <head>
            <title>Stripes By Example</title>
            <!-- CSS includes -->
            <!-- JavaScript includes -->
        </head>
        <body>
            <jsp:include page="./header.jsp" />
            <stripes:layout-component name="contents"/>
            <jsp:include page="./footer.jsp" />
        </body>
    </html>

</stripes:layout-definition>
```

Place your tag libs in another JSP file to avoid including them on every page.

Here we are defining a layout that will be used by other JSP pages.

See
<stripes:layout-component name="contents">
...
</stripes:layout-component>
in page1.jsp, page2.jsp, etc.

Listing 15-2. page1.jsp

```
<%@include file="basefiles/taglibs.jsp" %>
<stripes:layout-render name="./basefiles/base.jsp">
    <stripes:layout-component name="contents">

        ...Other html and JSTL code...

    </stripes:layout-component>
</stripes:layout-render>
```

Matches <stripes:layout-component name="contents"/> in base.jsp

As you can see in the two preceding JSP files, you are able to easily set up a `base.jsp` page, and multiple other JSPs that refer to it, and insert their contents into it.

Balance Your ActionBeans

Let's say that you had a requirement to manage orders in your application. You need the ability to create, delete, edit, and view orders. You could tackle this in two ways. You could create four action beans: `CreateOrderActionBean.java`, `DeleteOrderActionBean.java`, `EditOrderActionBean.java`, and `ViewOrdersActionBean.java`. Or, you could create `OrdersActionBean.java`, which contains fields and methods for each individual task.

Either of these options is valid and is up to personal preference. I, personally, like to keep all features contained in a single ActionBean unless it grows too large. For example, if there were multiple methods and parameters used to query an order, I might create `OrdersManagerActionBean.java` (to create, edit, and delete), and `OrdersQueryActionBean.java` (to select/view data).

The point is to find what works best for you and your application.

Returning Resolutions via Method Calls

You can leverage existing methods by returning the value from another method call. Listing 15-3 shows an example.

Listing 15-3. Method Delegation

```
@HandlesEvent("login")
public Resolution login(){
  boolean loginSuccess = userDAO.login(username, password);

  Resolution resolution = null;

  if(loginSuccess){
    resolution = new RedirectResolution(ApplicationMenuActionBean.class);
  } else {
    resolution = this.index();
  }
  return resolution;
}
```

This can save a lot of extra coding time and increase security, because redirecting to another ActionBean/method using via `RedirectResolution` either discards the values you have set in your ActionBean, or passes them to the browser in the URL if `includeRequestParameters(true)` is used, which could expose sensitive data.

Remember Your Tiers

Simply put, don't perform your business logic in an ActionBean. Delegate to some type of business object layer. Stripes' purpose is that of a web framework. It handles interactions between client and server. Find other means for your advanced business logic, such as Spring, EJBs, or even POJOs (Plain Old Java Objects) in their own package.

Separating your application into multiple layers has many advantages, such as keeping each piece smaller and easier to understand, not tying your application to a specific solution, making your code easier to refactor, and making each part easier to Unit Test.

Review

Becoming good at something doesn't happen overnight. No amount of reading will make you an expert (except maybe at history or law—*yawn*). Take the suggestions from this chapter and expand on them yourself as you begin to write more and more Java applications.

CHAPTER 16

Next Steps

It's hard to leave things out of a book. A book like this could easily be double or triple its size. The 80/20 rule (the Pareto Principle) is what I have tried to follow by covering the most commonly used parts of the Stripes framework. In doing so, I hope to have given you the best time-to-value ratio. Hopefully, you have been able to quickly consume this book and are now able to apply what you have learned.

Now for my suggestions on what to do next. First, and most importantly, is to put what you learned into practice (*What I hear, I forget. What I see, I remember. What I do, I understand.* —Lao Tse, Chinese philosopher). This, of course, means writing code. Either build something on your own or suggest the framework to your employer for your next project. The more Stripes applications you write, the more proficient you will become with it.

Don't be afraid of the Stripes source code. I suggest downloading the Stripes source code jar file (`stripes-x.x.x-sources.jar`) and configuring your IDE to allow browsing it. At times it helps to be able to click a Stripes class to see how it actually works. The source code is very well written, with lots of Javadoc. Becoming familiar with the Stripes web site is also very advantageous. The documentation is very robust and thorough. In addition to learning materials and extra examples, the web site also has a section dedicated to user contributions. These examples can be time-savers.

And, last but not least, if you find Stripes as enjoyable and productive as I have, let others know about it!

Brent Watson, *Stripes by Example*, DOI 10.1007/978-1-4842-0980-6_16

Index

Brent Watson, *Stripes by Example*, DOI 10.1007/978-1-4842-0980-6

E

F, G

H

I

J, K

L

M

N, O

P, Q

R

S

T

U

V, W, X, Y, Z